D1600781

The Glorious Ordinary

Discover the Hidden Glory of an Ordinary Life

Tim Ferguson

Checkerspot Studio LLC

The Glorious Ordinary
©2019 Checkerspot Studio LLC
All Rights Reserved
ISBN# 978-0-9896650-6-3
April 2019

I dedicate this book
To the generous and kind congregations
I served as pastor.
So much of my ministry, I realize now,
Was done in the weakness of the flesh.
I pray, whatever wounds I caused,
That you would find healing in this book,
A message born not of the flesh
But of the Spirit

May Jesus Christ fill your hearts
To overflowing

Contents

Acknowledgments

I wrote this book under the sustaining influence of Christian friends who offered their prayers, encouragement, and valuable feedback. Thank you, Esther P, Ruth Ann and Chuck N, Dianne J, Elaine M, Eric B, Teresa B, Mary G, Doris J, Frank and Fran M, Lisa B, Clyde and Arlene S, Chris D, and Bob C. And thank you, Carrie H, for an excellent editing job. (Any mistakes in the book are likely my fault, not yours.) And thanks to Bill and Joyce B; I'm blessed to have such great in-laws. And thanks as well to Keith W, fellow writer, for the ongoing moral support.

Finally, thank you to my wife Megan who has been a wonderful companion throughout this whole journey. Little did she know she married a guy who still hasn't figured out what he wants to do when (if?) he grows up. I love you, and I'm glad we're on this adventure together.

Sincerely,
Tim Ferguson
Pittsburgh, PA
March 2019

Part 1
A Return to the Simple Life

*Doing what is righteous and just
is more acceptable to the Lᴏʀᴅ than sacrifice.*

-Proverbs 21:3
(HCSB)

Chapter 1

The Glimmer of Hope

Where in the world did we get the idea that God requires everyone to serve him in big and impressive ways? I've known teachers in the church who come right out and say it: Unless you enter full-time ministry—such as becoming a pastor or a missionary— you're settling for second-best with God.

Such a lofty view of the Christian life sounds spiritual (in a weird sort of way), but it leaves a lot us feeling left out. What about the ordinary Christian with ordinary talents who never heard God call him to do anything extraordinary with his life? Or the Christian who tried to do something exceptional but bombed out? They're left wondering, "Lord, do my life and my accomplishments amount to much in your eyes? Are you disappointed in me? Why am I cursed with such a dull existence?" While other servants of God are moving mountains to great applause, our "ordinary Christian" is relegated to being a mere spectator in the church pew.

And he's not the only one feeling like a second-class servant of the Lord. Let's walk a few blocks to a nearby church where God's gifted servants are speaking in tongues, uttering prophetic messages, and sharing amazing testimonies about how God has been working in their lives. But seated quietly in the sanctuary are those who wonder why they can't duplicate these amazing works in their own lives. "Why don't I have an amazing story to tell?" they wonder. "Where are *my* miraculous gifts? Is there something wrong with my faith? Why is my life so darn ordinary?"

And let's not forget the men and women who, years ago, heard God's call to do something extraordinary. They laid it all on the altar when they were young, committing to a lifetime of kingdom service. They chose to become pastors, missionaries, youth leaders, or leaders of parachurch organizations. But, for reasons they still don't understand, the glorious road to kingdom-greatness took a detour, leaving them in the land of broken dreams. Now they're numbered among God's dropouts. "Lord, did I let you down? I thought you had called me to something exceptional. Did I misunderstand you? Was my faith too small? Was my vision too small?"

Others had different aspirations: "I wanted to be a successful Christian businessman." Or "I was going to write a Christian book." Or "I aspired to be a pioneer in Christian cinema." Or "Our worship band was poised to go bigtime." Despite all their noble intentions, the vision never materialized. Now, they're shackled to an ordinary life, and memories of lost opportunity keep them awake at night.

So, here we are, a whole bunch of us living in the shadow of God's disappointment. Our stories differ in the details, but we all have this in common: We're God's third-string team sitting on the bench. From the sidelines, we watch Christians more talented and more committed than we are take the field to play the big game. We dare not look our coach in the eye for fear of what we'll see— his disappointment. "I expected more from you," he'd say. "You had so much promise. What happened?"

Is that where you find yourself these days, on God's third-string? Are you stuck with an ordinary life or an ordinary ministry that you regard as uninspiring? Do you fear God remains unimpressed with your efforts?

Now, let me ask you another question: Are you ready for some good news? More than that, are you ready for some fantastic news? If so, listen closely. With a heartful of kindness, your Heavenly Father invites you to lay down that awful burden you've been carrying, that restless striving to do something big and impressive for him. And in return, he wants to satisfy your hunger for significance and lavish you with generous helpings of joy in your relationship with him.

For a long time now, you've wondered whether your life will ever amount to much in heaven's eyes. The truth is, the glory you long for is closer than you ever imagined, all gift-wrapped in the Gospel message. It's now time, finally, to open your eyes and see what has been true of you all along: *In the Kingdom of God there is no such thing as an ordinary life.* You are not (and never were) a third-string player on God's bench.

When the blood of our savior Jesus Christ washed all over you, you became a member of his royal family. And the Lord lifted you up to cosmic heights and imparted to you a glorious future full of hope, promise, and significance. Jesus, you see, brings purpose to everything. He brings bigness to the little things. *He brings glory to the ordinary.* No exceptions. No disclaimers. Again, let me ask you: Are you ready for good news?

A Surprising Discovery

The Glorious Ordinary is a message the Lord gave me during a long and arduous personal journey. I'll tell you my story a little later. For now, all you need to know is this: A few years ago, all my plans to serve the Lord in a big way hit a wall. I had to say goodbye to my kingdom-dreams and settle for the curse of an ordinary life: Go to work, bring home a paycheck, take care of the family, fix up the house, go to church—Lather. Rinse. Repeat—until I die. Finally, I slink into heaven and apologize for wasting the only life God had given me.

Then one day, I caught a glimmer of hope in an unassuming verse of Scripture. "Make it your goal to live a quiet life," writes the apostle Paul, "minding your own business and working with your hands, just as we instructed you before." (1 Thessalonians 4:11, NLT) Wow, did you just do a double-take? I did, figuratively, when I discovered that verse. It seemed God was telling me to devote myself to a quiet, ordinary life. I was intrigued. Was God calling me to be an underachiever? Let's be honest. The passage does not make for a dramatic altar call at church. When was the last time you heard a preacher implore the congregation to come forward and commit themselves to a quiet life?

Let's examine the verse phrase by phrase, just to make sure. **"Make it your goal..."** I love statements like that in the Bible. The Lord is about to reveal what he wants me to do. He's given me a target. I need that. Purpose! Clarity! Boil it down for me!

"To live a quiet life..." So, an unassuming life is something God actually desires for his people? If I never rise to celebrity-status in the kingdom—maybe that's okay after all?

"Minding your own business..." In other words, don't be a busybody. Stop prying into other people's affairs. Not a lot of theological complexity there.

"Working with your hands..." A little background helps at this point. Some Christians in the Thessalonian church were drifters, able-bodied people unwilling to get a job to support themselves. Instead, they leeched off their fellow Christians. For Paul, that was unacceptable. Enough, he told them. It's time to work with your hands. Don't be afraid to get your hands dirty. Dirt's not beneath you, but laziness is. So, we learn God is pleased with dirty hands. What's more ordinary than that?

Finally, the last part of the verse: "**Just as we instructed you before.**" Clearly this was not the first time Paul had given this admonition. It was a common refrain in his teaching: *This is God's will for you: Live a quiet life. Don't be a busybody. Go to work. Provide for yourself and your family, and if that means getting your hands dirty, then get your hands dirty.*

So, there it is, a verse where God commands his people to lead what looks like a very ordinary life. This surprising passage raises all sorts of questions: Is it possible there's more to the ordinary life than meets the eye? Is there heavenly glory stored up for the Christian who faithfully lives out his ordinary life? Might he one day hear his Heavenly Father say, "Well done, good and faithful servant"? (Matthew 25:21)

I'm convinced the answer to all those questions, based on the clear voice of Scripture, is a resounding "Yes!" And *The Glorious Ordinary* is all about helping you hear that liberating message. In fact, here's a sneak-peek of what's ahead: The transformation from the misery of an ordinary life to the joy of a significant life requires opening our eyes and seeing the glory around us, glory that's been there all along.

Think of it this way: When Jesus inaugurated his official ministry on earth, he announced to his countrymen, "The kingdom of heaven *has come near!*" (Matthew 4:17, HCSB) In other words, the glory of God's Kingdom stood right in their midst, but many missed seeing him because the King of Glory appeared as a dusty, itinerant preacher with dirt under his fingernails. Those who touched him were touching the one who created the heavens and the earth, yet they had no idea.

Your life is a lot like that. The glory of God's kingdom has come near, and it is camouflaged by the dust-covered ordinary. You simply need to open your eyes and see the splendor. If all this sounds like theological make-believe, I assure you it's not. You will find, in the pages ahead, a practical guide on how to invite heaven's glory to fill the most mundane moments of your day, all according to the amazing invitations we find in Scripture.

But our journey won't stop there. We'll dig down further until we get to the heart of this angst to do big things for God. Many of us will discover, deep down, we harbor a distorted view of the Lord. We're convinced his love is results-driven. To put it another way, we believe God loves us to the extent he finds us useful. But nothing could be further from the truth. Your Heavenly Father loves you simply because you're his dear child, and his love is rich with affection. You don't have to win him over. You already have his heart.

Can I let you in on a secret? For a long, long time, I was one of those third-string players sitting on God's bench. A few years ago, once the message of *The Glorious Ordinary* finally made a home in my heart, I dared to look our coach in the eye, and to my wonderful surprise, I didn't see disappointment.

I saw delight.

I saw pleasure.

In me.

And he delights in you, too. But don't take my word for it. Take his. We'll find that message all through Scripture. And rest assured, the Holy Spirit longs to pour that loving message into your heart (Romans 5:5). That's what this book is all about, helping you see God's glory in the ordinary stuff of life and experience his pleasure along the way. I'm excited you're coming along on the journey. Let's begin.

Chapter 2
Keeping it Simple

"Lord, what is your will for my life? What do you require of me? How do I know when I've given enough?" People have been asking those questions for millennia. The answers, we'll soon discover, are surprisingly simple—and liberating! They always have been.

The problem is human nature which has a penchant for turning something simple into something terribly complicated. Case in point, over the last two thousand years, people have layered a lot of complexity onto the teachings of Jesus. In fact, many of us find the Christian life so burdensome, we cannot fathom what Jesus meant when he said, "Come to Me, all of you who are weary and burdened, and I will give you rest." (Matthew 11:28, HCSB)

Manmade religious complexity was already a severe problem in Jesus' day. Scholars had twisted the Law of Moses into a byzantine system of requirements only a lawyer could love. But Jesus, who came to bring freedom to the oppressed, condemned those who trafficked in cruel dogma. "They crush people with unbearable religious demands," he said, "and never lift a finger to ease the burden." (Matthew 23:4, NLT)

But Jesus went even further. In a single masterstroke, he swept away all that convoluted doctrine and replaced it with an easy-to-remember summary of the godly life, one so simple a child could grasp it. Believe it or not, Jesus took all of Scripture (Genesis through Malachi in that day) and reduced it to .01% of the original—from 23,000 verses to three!

Here's how it happened. During one of Jesus' public appearances, a religious scribe asked him a question. This scribe, unlike his scheming colleagues, seemed to be a genuine seeker of truth. "Which command is the most important of all?" the scribe asked. And here is how Jesus replied:

> "This is the most important," Jesus answered: "'Listen, Israel! The Lord our God, the Lord is One. Love the Lord your God with all your heart, with all your soul, with all your mind, and with all your strength.' The second is: Love your neighbor as yourself. There is no other command greater than these."

> (Mark 12:28-31, HCSB)

All 23,000 verses of the Old Testament, says Jesus, hang on those two commandments (Matthew 22:40). Amazing. Jesus has distilled the godly life to its essence: Love God with your whole being and love your neighbor as yourself. Got it? Try not to overthink it. Don't make it more complicated than it really is.

Now, before we rush off to apply what we've learned, let's return to the dialogue between Jesus and this teacher because their final exchange is insightful.

Then the scribe said to [Jesus], "You are right, Teacher! You have correctly said that He is One, and there is no one else except Him. And to love Him with all your heart, with all your understanding, and with all your strength, and to love your neighbor as yourself, is far more important than all the burnt offerings and sacrifices."

When Jesus saw that he answered intelligently, He said to him, "You are not far from the kingdom of God."

(Mark 12:32-34, HCSB)

Did you catch the man's amazing observation? Obedience to those two simple commands— love God and love your neighbor—was more pleasing to the Lord than performing all the rituals and ceremonies prescribed in the Law of Moses. And Jesus commended the man's insight.

Here we find a theme that emerges from Scripture time and again. God is not looking for the big and impressive sacrifice from his people. He longs for something much simpler: That we love him and that we love our neighbor. Jesus' sense of priority is needed just as much today. We must allow Jesus to come into our lives and clean house of all the nonessential stuff that clutters our relationship with God. Love God with your whole being—heart, soul, mind, and strength. And love your neighbor as yourself.

Love God. Love people.

Wonderful simplicity.

Now, some of you wonder how any of this is good news. Jesus' summary of the godly life, though succinct, remains incredibly challenging. God requires us to love him with our whole being. That's no walk in the park.

Indeed, loving God is a high calling, to say the least, but I wonder if our anxiety stems from a misunderstanding. Have we assumed God only accepts big and dramatic expressions of love? In other words, to prove my love for the Lord, must I search for a Goliath to slay as David did? Must I commit to the mission field as the apostle Paul did? Must I build an altar and offer my firstborn as Abraham did?

I admit, this impulse to lay something big and costly on God's altar makes a lot of sense. After all, God is worthy of our highest and best. Why should we offer anything less? But there's a problem. As I listen to God's voice in Scripture, I hear him saying something very different. He's not demanding the big and costly sacrifice or that we try and impress him with our big kingdom accomplishments.

Uh, oh. Have I just veered into heresy? Some of you suspect I have, so let me be clear about something: If God ever calls me to go up against Goliath, I pray I'll have David's courage. If he calls me to the mission field, I pray I'll go with Paul's zeal. And if he commands me to lay my son on the altar, I pray I'll embody Abraham's faith. But—and this is the important part—for most of us, most of the time, we will express our supreme love for God by our devotion to very ordinary-looking responsibilities. That's worth repeating:

> *For most of us, most of the time,*
> *We will express our supreme love for God*
> *By our devotion to very ordinary-looking responsibilities.*

At first glance, that appears to be a contradiction. How can we express *supreme love* through *ordinary acts of obedience*? Are the two concepts even compatible? Yes, they are. In fact, when you think about it, they exist in perfect harmony in the marriage relationship. Let me explain.

God is the grand architect of marriage, and he calls on the husband to reserve his highest love for his wife. That is, among human relationships, he must love no one else more than he loves his wife. In fact, the man ought to love his bride as much as Christ loved his. The bride of Christ, we learn from Scripture, is the church, and Jesus loved her so much, he gave his very life for her. (See Ephesians 5:25-33.) Jesus' supreme expression of love is the husband's standard. Without a doubt, God raised the bar as high as it will go.

As a husband, that gives me a lot to think about. Jesus died for his bride. Am I willing to die for mine? Suppose I'm in the big city one night, walking hand-in-hand with my wife Megan. By accident, we turn into a dark alley. Suddenly a masked gunman leaps from the shadows and raises his pistol. At that moment, my love is put to the test. Do I love Megan enough to take the bullet for her? Will I lay down my life for my bride as Christ did for his?

I pray to God my love for Megan would pass the bullet test. That said, I have a confession to make: I don't spend a lot of time in dark alleys hoping to prove the heights of my love. Honestly, showing love to Megan most days requires my commitment to more modest responsibilities: By being a tenderhearted listener; by setting a good example in the home; by showing affection; by helping her carry the load when she's tired; by arranging my priorities to protect our relationship—and the list goes on. I see a similar dynamic in my love for the Lord. Much of my obedience will happen in the everyday goings-on of life, not the headline-making sacrifices.

The prophet Micah, seven centuries before Jesus, made this very point. The Israelites of his generation were asking the same questions we ask today: "What does God want from us? How big a sacrifice does he require?" Hear for yourself what people were asking:

> What can we bring to the LORD?
>   Should we bring him burnt offerings?
> Should we bow before God Most High
>   with offerings of yearling calves?

> Should we offer him thousands of rams
>   and ten thousand rivers of olive oil?
> Should we sacrifice our firstborn children
>   to pay for our sins?

(Micah 6:6–7, NLT)

Just like many Christians today, the Israelites assumed God required extraordinary sacrifices: "A thousand rams! Ten thousand rivers of oil! Our firstborn children!" Sound familiar? Notice, though, how God replies: "No, O people, the LORD has told you what is good, and this is what he requires of you: to do what is right, to love mercy, and to walk humbly with your God." (Micah 6:8, NLT)

It turns out God was not seeking the colossal acts of devotion after all. He simply wanted his people to return to the basic commands he had already given them: *Do what is right. Love mercy. Walk humbly with God.* In other words, apply God's goodness, his integrity, and his compassion to the ordinary stuff of life. And God desires this as well, that we walk humbly with him. To walk with God is a picture of obedience and personal relationship, a winsome invitation we'll revisit in the pages ahead.

Even today, when people cry to heaven in search of God's will, his answer remains the same. What the Lord desires is far simpler and far more accessible than most of us realize. Again, people tend to make things complicated, but God brings simplicity. And in that simplicity, we find joyous liberty.

So, are you feeling a little lighter? I hope so. Remember, Jesus did not come to weigh us down with additional burdens. He brings good news to the weary. And we're just getting started. The good news only gets better.

Chapter 3

All of Life a Sanctuary

My transition from high school to college was a time of high anxiety. I was overwhelmed at all the life-altering decisions barreling toward me at once: What career will I choose? Where will I go to college? What should I study? Should I move away from home? And as a young Christian with a desire to serve the Lord, I faced other pressing questions as well: Should I go into full-time ministry? How do I determine God's will? Is there such a thing as a call to ministry?

I realize now that behind all my turmoil was the youthful ambition to make a difference with my life. For me, that meant doing something extraordinary for the Lord. I wanted to put something big and dramatic on his altar. What I lacked, though, was a clear understanding of what he wanted. Then, all of a sudden, God came to my rescue. He spoke to me so vividly through a single verse of Scripture, it seemed the Holy Spirit had whispered right in my ear.

The message arrived one evening during our family devotions. As was customary, my mom corralled the family into the living room after dinner. One of us would read a chapter of the New Testament while everyone else listened—or at least pretended to. That night, it was my turn to read, so I opened the Bible where we had left off, and I immediately discovered these words written by the apostle Paul:

> Therefore I urge you, brethren, by the mercies of God, to present your bodies a living and holy sacrifice, acceptable to God, which is your spiritual service of worship.

(Romans 12:1, NASB)

The verse seized my attention. Intuitively, I knew this was the answer to all my anxiety, as though God were kindly tapping his finger on the page and saying, "*This* is the kind of sacrifice I desire from you. *This* is your spiritual service of worship." The revelation was so clear, I welled with laughter, and that earned some strange looks from my family. But I regained my composure long enough to keep reading. As I waded deeper into the chapter, each verse opened like a beautiful flower, offering insight into God's will for my life.

So, what in the world did I see in Romans 12:1?

God was calling me to present my body to him as "a living and holy sacrifice." I knew the sacrifice-imagery hearkened back to the Law of Moses, something quite familiar to the first-century Jews in Paul's audience. Under the Law, a worshiper expressed his devotion to God by visiting the temple in Jerusalem and laying gifts on the altar, perhaps an animal sacrifice from his herd or a grain sacrifice from his harvest. Those ceremonies served as living prophecies, if you will, all pointing to Jesus Christ's sacrifice on the cross.

Because Jesus' death and resurrection fulfilled the purpose of the ceremonial law, the ancient system of animal sacrifices became obsolete (Hebrews 8:13). That raised an important question for the early Christians: Without the temple and the altar, how does a worshiper express his devotion to God? Using the sacrifice-on-the-altar metaphor, Paul explains in Romans 12:1 what God desires. Allow me to illuminate his point through an imaginary dialogue between Paul and a young protégé.

"Now that I'm a Christian," says the young protégé, "I want my life to count for God. What does he want from me?"

Paul replies, "He wants you to present your body to him as a living and holy sacrifice."

"Excuse me? Are you talking about instituting human sacrifices — like the Aztecs?!"

"No, no, no. It's a figure of speech. God desires a *living* sacrifice, not a dead sacrifice. Present your body to the Lord as a *living* sacrifice."

"I'm still unclear. Is there an altar somewhere I need to climb onto?"

"Remember English class? Remember the lesson on metaphors?"

"The altar is a metaphor?"

"Exactly. Present your body to the Lord as something that is holy and acceptable."

The protégé stammers. "Uh..."

"Still need help?"

"Yes, please."

"Whenever the Lord looks at your body, he wants to see it behaving in a manner that is holy and pleasing to him."

"Like going to church and attending Bible study!"

"Yes, but it involves much more than that. Let me ask you: When you went to work this morning, did you take your body with you?"

"Of course."

"When you had dinner with your family, where was your body?"

"My body was right there with me."

"Do you ever go anywhere without your body?"

"Of course not."

"So, God's command affects every moment of your life, doesn't it? No matter what you're doing, conduct yourself in a manner that is holy. God will accept it as a personal gift, and he'll be pleased— whether you're at home, in church, at work, or playing with your children."

"Interesting. So, what does it mean 'to live in a way that is holy?'"

"Your behavior, your attitudes, and your words should conform to God's holy character. Let your life become a continual expression of his love, his integrity, his purity, and his kindness. There are no limits. Anything you do—*anything*—do it in a manner that reflects the beauty of God's character. That makes him very happy."

"Wow, Paul, you're great at explaining things. Have you considered writing a book?"

"Actually, I've written several."

I still remember, over thirty years later, that eureka-discovery. One moment I was stressed out over finding God's will for my life, and the next moment it all became clear: I am to live out his holy character in whatever I'm doing, right here and right now. God's will, I realized, was less about *what* I'm supposed to do with my life and more about *how* I do the thing I'm doing right now. What beautiful simplicity.

That one verse, Romans 12:1, bestows glorious potential to every moment of every day. As a matter of fact, we have just discovered a seminal truth which will transform your dull Christian life into one that is inspiring: *God's perfect will for you is always within your reach. Always. Every moment of every day.* The apostle Peter echoes this very same truth: "**Be holy in everything you do**, just as God who chose you is holy." (1 Peter 1:14-15, NLT) Again, it's all about bringing holiness to *everything* we do—including the very ordinary things we are doing already.

So, on a practical level, how do we embody Romans 12:1? What does it mean to be holy in everything we do? *The Glorious Ordinary* is all about answering those questions. In fact, the chapters ahead are brimming with practical help. In the meantime, Romans 12 provides all sorts of admonitions to spur us on toward godly living, offering a beautiful portrait of what it means to present our bodies as living and holy sacrifices. Allow me to paraphrase the highlights:

Do not let the world squeeze you into its mold (Romans 12:2).

Transform your mind to God's way of thinking (v.2).

Stay humble. Don't be overly impressed with yourself (v.3).

Use whatever talent you have (big or small) to serve God's people for their benefit (vv.4-8).

Make sure your love for others is genuine, not phony (v.9).

Show affection toward your church family (v.10).

Treat others with honor and dignity (v.10).

Serve the Lord with enthusiasm (v.11).

Be filled with joy, with hope, and with patience in all circumstances (v.12).

Be devoted to prayer (v.12).

Share with those who are in need (v.13).

Welcome people warmly into your home (v.13).

Be sympathetic. Share in the joys of others. And share in their tears as well (v.15).

Live in harmony with others (v.16).

Never view anyone as beneath you. Never be conceited (v.16).

Don't get even with the difficult people. Let God deal with them (v.19).

Choose to be a blessing to the people in your life who least deserve it (vv.20-21).

What an elegant expression of God's will for my life. Whether I'm at work, at home, or on the ballfield, I can be humble, I can show genuine love, I can show joy, I can show hope, I can cultivate harmony in my relationships, and I can treat others with dignity. The Christian life, as it turns out, is incredibly portable.

All of Life a Sanctuary

Now, let's take a second look at Romans 12:1 because there's another gem hidden in plain sight. See if you can spot it: "Therefore I urge you, brethren, by the mercies of God, to present your bodies a living and holy sacrifice, acceptable to God, which is your spiritual service of worship." (NASB)

Did you find the gem? It's the very last word, *worship*. In other words, during those very ordinary moments at home, at work, or at the grocery store, when you choose to conduct yourself in a manner that conforms to God's character, God accepts your offering as *worship*.

Yes, worship.

Jesus Christ has transformed you into a living sanctuary. Don't miss the implication: God never intended for you to divide your life into sacred activities and secular activities. To the contrary, every moment of your life is sacred because the blood of Jesus Christ has made you sacred. You are a member of God's "holy [or *sacred*] nation." (1 Peter 2:9) And he calls you to live accordingly.

We must banish from our thoughts the secular-versus-sacred way of thinking, thoughts like these: *If I'm a pastor, I'm in sacred work, but if I'm a software engineer, I'm in secular work. If I'm a missionary, I'm in sacred work, but if I'm a bricklayer, I'm in secular work. Going to church is a spiritual activity, but cleaning the house is secular activity.* Wrong, wrong, wrong, wrong! That kind of thinking is the exact opposite of what God intended. He calls us to transform every moment of the day into worship, not just the hour on Sunday when we're gathered in the church building.

Think of it this way: When Jesus walked the dusty streets of Galilee and Judea, he was the embodiment of God's word. As John wrote in his gospel, "And the Word became flesh, and dwelt among us." (John 1:14, NASB) In much the same way, God calls you to embody his word in your own corner of the world. Be Jesus in your neighborhood. Paul expressed it this way, "Put on the Lord Jesus Christ." (Romans 13:14, HCSB) That is, wear Jesus like a suit. Live out his wonderful love and holiness right where you are.

Are you beginning to see how significance in God's kingdom is always within your reach? If you're a bricklayer, show the world how Jesus builds a wall. If you're a mom managing the home, show the world how Jesus changes a diaper. (Don't worry that no one is around to see you. Heaven is watching.) The possibilities are endless: This is how Jesus changes the oil in his car. This is how Jesus mows the lawn. This is how Jesus plays soccer. This is how Jesus relaxes and has a good time ... on and on and on. Suddenly, the ordinary activities of everyday life shine with heaven's glory.

And God receives it all as *worship.*

Live in the Present

As marvelous as Romans 12:1 has been so far, we still haven't plumbed all its blessings. There's more rich goodness for us to enjoy, and it relates to the age-old question, "Lord, what's your will for my life?"

As I mentioned already, when I first discovered Romans 12, I was in turmoil over discerning God's leading: *Does the Lord want me to go into vocational ministry? Which college should I attend? Should I go to seminary?* Many of you can relate because it's a common anxiety among Christians. Worst of all, some of you fear you chose badly at a crucial juncture and now you're fated to live outside God's will the rest of your days.

When it comes to figuring out God's plan for our lives, I believe Scripture is far more optimistic than we are. In fact, Romans 12 ought to embolden our optimism. Remember, in Romans 12:1 the Lord has already revealed his will for your life: Embody his wonderful character right where you are— right here and right now. Stay in the moment, as the saying goes.

Then, in the verse immediately following, God makes a promise regarding your future: If you choose to live in the moment and embrace the Lord's will right where you are, you will grow more and more in tune with his leading. That is, "...You will learn to know God's will for you, which is good and pleasing and perfect." (Romans 12:2, NLT)

Think of it. God invites you to live out his will right here and right now. That's the heart of Romans 12:1. In return, he will grant you deeper insight into his long-term plan for your life. That's the heart of 12:2. This is a gradual process that requires trust and patience, but rest assured, your insight into God's ways will grow in clarity. All of this echoes a proverb familiar to many: "In all your ways acknowledge [the Lord], and He shall direct your paths." (Proverbs 3:6, KJV)

To be clear, I am not suggesting we disregard long-term planning. All of us, from time to time, will wrestle through decisions which affect the course of our lives. But Romans 12:1-2 keeps the matter in proper perspective. It helps us escape the misguided anxiety that making a wrong decision today will leave me forever outside God's will. The fact remains, God's will is always within my reach. His will encompasses what I'm facing right here and right now. If that remains my priority, God will keep me on the path he has marked out for my life.

That's why the message of *The Glorious Ordinary* is for everyone, even for those of you called by God to serve in extra-ordinary ways, as a pastor or as a missionary for example. Contrary to what some fear, choosing to be faithful in small things *now* in your present situation will *not* lead you to a dead end. Rather, it will lead you to God's good and perfect will as per Romans 12:2. In fact, God watches how we handle the ordinary to determine when we are ready for the extra-ordinary. "If you are faithful in little things," says Jesus, "you will be faithful in large ones ... And if you are untrustworthy about worldly wealth, who will trust you with the true riches of heaven?" (Luke 16:10-11, NLT)

In discussing their golf game, players will refer to their short game (chipping onto the green and putting) and their long game (long shots down the fairway). Life also has a short and a long game, and we are learning how important it is for the Christian to play the short game well. In return, God assures us he has his eye on the long game.

And God is immensely qualified to handle your long game. He knows your final destination and has already determined how he'll get you there. Even before you were born, he mapped out exactly how you would serve him. "For we are God's masterpiece," Paul writes in Ephesians. "He has created us anew in Christ Jesus, so we can do the good things he planned for us long ago." (2:10, NLT)

Often, when Christians discover Ephesians 2:10, they wonder how they're supposed to figure out what good works God prepared them to do. But that misses the whole point! The verse is not a puzzle to solve; it's a promise to embrace. Our life-purpose is safe in God's hands. Frankly, the mystery of Ephesians 2:10 is beyond human understanding. Just believe it and enjoy it. God gave you that verse for your encouragement.

Remember, if God's eye is on the sparrow, his eye is certainly on you, his beloved child (Luke 12:6-7). When it's time to move you to your next assignment, your Heavenly Father knows where to find you. If he needs to recruit a giant fish to get you back on track, he will. Just ask Jonah the prophet. If all those stories in the Bible teach us anything, it's this: God is remarkably good at getting his servants where they need to be—even when the servant has no idea what God is up to in his life, which seems to be the case most of the time.

Keep your eye on the short game and trust your Heavenly Father. He's the master of the long game.

Wings to Soar, Freedom to Fail

So, how are you feeling so far? Excited? Relieved? Or are you dealing with a tinge of performance anxiety? Perhaps you're thinking, *Is all this really such good news? God expects me to live up to the holy standards of Jesus—every moment of the day? Are you kidding me? Seriously?!*

Indeed, God has placed a huge challenge before us, to embody the loving and holy character of Jesus Christ wherever we go. It's an enormous undertaking, and speaking personally, I've stumbled many times during the journey. But I'm not discouraged. I've learned to stand up, brush myself off, and press on with confidence. And you should, too. You have every reason to move forward in the spirit of victory. Here's why.

Did you notice that Romans 12:1 begins with the word "therefore"? That means Romans 12 is the natural outflow of all the preceding chapters. We cannot fully understand the spirit of Romans 12 unless we grasp all the good news which came before. The NIV, in fact, renders 12:1 this way: "Therefore, I urge you, brothers and sisters, *in view of God's mercy* ..." In other words, we are to read Romans 12 with God's mercy in view, and God's mercy is on full display in the preceding eleven chapters. Here are just a few highlights for your encouragement, to ease your performance anxiety.

"For all have sinned and fall short of the glory of God." (Romans 3:23, HCSB) Do you feel overwhelmed at God's high standards? That's normal and expected. Remember, if you had any chance of measuring up to God's standards on your own, there was no reason for Jesus to die on the cross (Galatians 2:21). God already knows you fall short. The fact you feel it in your heart is actually a good sign. It shows you're honest about your shortcomings. Good. God can use that. It's a mark of humility. That's why Jesus told his followers, "Blessed are the poor in spirit." (Matthew 5:3)

"They [all those poor sinners] are justified [declared righteous] *freely* by His grace through the redemption that is in Christ Jesus...For we conclude that a man is justified *by faith* apart from the works of the law." (3:24, 28, HCSB) Have you placed your faith in Jesus Christ? Then rejoice. God has already declared you righteous, the one requirement for you to enter his eternal kingdom.

Think of it this way: Life is a classroom, and you need a passing grade to enter heaven's glory. Here's the good news: God has already given you an *A* for the course because you have embraced his son Jesus Christ. You are now free to study, learn, and mature without fear of failure. If you bomb a test, get up, learn from your mistakes, and try again. The *A* on your report card remains unchanged, forever recorded in permanent ink. God will not erase your passing grade. So, go for it!

"Therefore, since we have been declared righteous by faith, we have peace with God through our Lord Jesus Christ." (5:1, HCSB) Breathe it in slowly like a fresh ocean breeze: *We have peace with God.* Through the loving sacrifice of Jesus Christ, the most important matter in your life has been resolved: The relationship between you and God is mended. God intended for you to enjoy peace and harmony with him. So, relax. He's your friend, not your adversary.

"For we know that our old self was crucified with Him in order that sin's dominion over the body may be abolished, so that we may no longer be enslaved to sin..." (6:6, HCSB) When Jesus came into your life, he transformed you from the inside out. You are not the same person you used to be. The old you "was crucified with Him." The brand new you is free from sin's dominion. Will you battle sin and temptation in the days ahead? Absolutely. Will you experience setbacks? Yes. But you can face these challenges with optimism because Jesus Christ has empowered you to rise above your old way of life. Sin no longer determines your destiny. Jesus Christ does. He is actively working to finish what he started in your life (Philippians 1:6).

"Therefore, *no condemnation* now exists for those in Christ Jesus." (8:1, HCSB) Another priceless blessing: Our relationship with our Heavenly Father is free of any condemnation.

Again, no condemnation. Has that truth taken root in your heart? Let me ask you: While reading these chapters, did you feel crushed by the ever-growing weight of condemnation? Did you feel defeated from the outset? As we reviewed Romans 12, perhaps the conversation in your head went something like this: *Live holy and pleasing to the Lord.* ["Failed."] *Serve the Lord with your talents.* ["What talents?!"] *Let your love be genuine.* ["How many times have I blown that one?"] By now, you're beaten black and blue.

So, who keeps rubbing your nose in all your failures? It's not God. God makes it clear: There is *no condemnation* in Christ Jesus. In fact, Jesus is cheering you on. Even better, he's lifting you up in earnest prayer: "Who dares accuse us whom God has chosen for his own? No one—for God himself has given us right standing with himself. Who then will condemn us? No one—for Christ Jesus died for us and was raised to life for us, and he is sitting in the place of honor at God's right hand, pleading [or *interceding*] for us." (Romans 8:33-34, NLT) Please notice: Jesus has your back. He's your advocate (1 John 2:1). He lifts you up in prayer, constantly. He wants you to succeed.

So again, who's condemning you? Perhaps the voices in your head are echoes from your past, people who incessantly criticized you and tore you down. Stop listening to them. Let your heart embrace what *God* has said about you.

Perhaps the harsh voice of judgment you hear belongs to the Devil. Scripture consistently portrays him as an accuser of God's people

(Revelation 12:10). And you can be sure he'll try to pass himself off as the voice of your Heavenly Father. Don't fall for it!

Possibly the condemning voice in your head belongs to you. You've become your own worst enemy. You extend patience and understanding to others, but you won't extend it to yourself. You never cut yourself a break. "But I can't cut myself a break," you cry. "God's standards are high! He demands so much!"

I agree. God's standards are high, but is he really demanding in spirit? Does he come to us barking orders, or does he come with a tender heart? I suggest it's the latter. Jesus described himself as "gentle and humble in heart," as one who offers rest for our souls (Matthew 11:28-30). Isaiah the prophet saw a glimpse of Jesus' tender spirit: "He will not shout or raise his voice in public. He will not crush the weakest reed or put out a flickering candle." (Isaiah 42:1-3, NLT) It takes a very gentle touch to mend a bruised reed without breaking it or to coax a flickering candle back to life without snuffing it out. Indeed, Jesus, the healer of our souls, ministers with a soft touch.

Earlier, I described the defeated Christian as a third-string player on the sidelines, demoralized as he watches the starting lineup play the game. Memories of all his dumb mistakes on the field haunt him. Thoroughly dejected, he turns to face the coach, unable to speak aloud the question on his heart, "You don't want me in the game, do you?" To his utter surprise, the coach walks over, slaps him on the back, and says, "Son, take the field."

"Take the field?!"

"Yes, take the field. Get in the game!"

And that's Jesus' invitation to you: Get in the game.

Every moment of your life, God hands you the ball and tells you to run for glory. Whatever you do, wherever you go, no moment is a small moment. It's bursting with potential glory. Offer your body as a living and holy sacrifice to God, and that moment is transformed into beautiful worship. Live out your days as Jesus would live them. Yes, you'll stumble, you'll fail, and you'll learn as you go. But that's okay. The coach isn't going to bench you. He'll tell you to get up, be honest about your mistakes, accept his forgiveness, and get back on the field. The glory is in the struggle.

Are you ready to get off the bench and take the field again? Then I have a suggestion: Open your Bible to Romans chapter twelve and read it aloud with your mind and your heart fully engaged. Don't rush. Soak it all in. Instead of condemning yourself as you read, be inspired.

Guys, do you remember when, as a kid, you saw your first fireman? You said to yourself, "I'm going to be a fireman one day." Ladies, what was your aspiration, to become a mom, a teacher, or a doctor? Whatever your childhood dream, bring that same spirit to Romans 12. Remember, those verses describe in beautiful simplicity the wonderful character of Jesus Christ. Be inspired. Be awed. Point to him and say, "I want to be just like him. I want to be that guy."

Now, go. Be Jesus. Rejoice that every moment in your life holds glorious significance. Your whole life is a sanctuary. Don't get hung up on failure. We all fail. And God is compassionate. Smile at the opportunities in front of you.

Too Good to Be True?

Are you finding all this Christ-centered optimism a little hard to swallow?

"Don't get hung up on failure?"

"God is compassionate?"

"Smile at the opportunities in front of me?"

If all this sounds too good to be true, I have an idea. Let's postpone any more talk about "the what," and let's talk about "the who." That is, let's move beyond *what* God wants us to do and become reacquainted with *who* he is. Let's rediscover the heart of our Heavenly Father.

Who is God really? How does he *feel* about us, his children? We know he loves us, but does he *like* us? Is he stern or is he gentle? Is he demanding or is he patient? Does he look at us with hope and optimism, or is he easily disappointed? Is he aloof or is he approachable? Does he enjoy his relationship with us or are we tools he finds useful?

How you answer those questions will, in a profound way, impact your walk with God. It will determine whether you serve him with a heartful of joy, a heartful of misery, or something in between. Really, the issue gets to the root of our performance anxiety in the Christian life. You see, it's not enough to know what God wants you to do. You must also understand his heart toward you, his beloved child.

During my high school and college years, I worked for my dad's construction company in the summer months. Because of my growing experience, I could jump right in and get to work, no matter which crew I was assigned to. Some crews, I discovered, were a pleasure to work with; others were miserable. What made the difference? Usually the foreman. Some foremen were courteous and supportive. Others were edgy and demanding. On every crew I performed the same work, but whether I enjoyed the work depended on who I was serving. Same work. Different boss. Big difference.

The same dynamic exists in our relationship with God. Two Christians can serve the Lord in identical ways, but one is miserable while the other is full of joy. One is never quite sure he's accomplished enough. The other experiences God's pleasure in even the smallest act of obedience. What's the difference? Each one has a very different view of God. Same work. Different boss. Big difference.

So, let me ask you: Who do you serve? If you're unsure how to answer, hold on for a wild ride. More good news is coming. In the next two chapters, allow me to introduce you all over again to the

God we serve. I invite you to draw near, rest your head against his bosom, and hear the heartbeat of your Heavenly Father. And listen closely. His heart beats for you.

Part 2
His Heart Beats for You

My lips will glorify You
because Your faithful love is better than life.

-King David
Psalm 63:3
(HCSB)

Chapter 4

A God Who Delights in You

God loves you because the Bible tells you so, right? But does he *like* you? Does he enjoy being with you? Are you special to him, or are you merely a tool he finds useful?

How you answer those questions will impact, for better or for worse, your relationship with your Heavenly Father. Unfortunately, a lot of Christians are convinced God's love is no more than a utilitarian thing. They grew up on a diet of teaching that went something like this: "God's love for you has nothing to do with feelings. He chose you for salvation based on reasons no one understands. That's all you need to know. He doesn't care if you're happy. He just wants you to be holy. If you were looking for something more personal, you're falling prey to emotionalism. Just accept the fact God loves you and be thankful you're not going to hell."

Is that the same God who inspired John Newton to pen the beautiful hymn "Amazing Grace"? It's hard to believe so. Thankfully, God's love is so much more than we can imagine. He does not love us merely because we are useful to him. He loves us because—Well, that's the mystery of God's love, isn't it? It's like trying to explain a mother's love for her child. It's a love that mere words cannot express. A mother's love, yes, is about commitment and sacrifice. But it's also about affection and genuine emotion.

That kind of heartfelt love is a reflection of God's love for his people. This comes from no higher authority than the Bible itself. Consider the poignant image of Psalm 131, a song penned by David as the Holy Spirit guided him:

> LORD, my heart is not proud;
>   my eyes are not haughty.
> I do not get involved with things
>   too great or too difficult for me.
> Instead, I have calmed and quieted myself
>   like a little weaned child with its mother;
> I am like a little child.
>
> Israel, put your hope in the LORD,
>   both now and forever.
>
> (Psalm 131, HCSB)

When David looked for an image to convey his relationship with the Lord, he chose that of a young child curled in the arms of his mother. Notice the child is weaned; he no longer seeks milk from his mother. Instead, he simply desires being with her, not what he can get from her. In her tender embrace, he has calmed and quieted himself, safe and content in her arms.

At such a young age, there is nothing the child can *do* for his mother. In fact, the relationship in those early years is all about mom doing for the child: bottles, diapers, baths, feeding, burping, and on and on. And yet nothing is more precious to mom than those quiet moments holding and rocking her child in perfect contentment. All that affection, all that warmth has nothing to do with what her child has *done* for her lately. In Psalm 131 the child is *enjoying* his mom, and the mom is *enjoying* her child.

Psalm 131 is a picture of God *enjoying* you.

When was the last time you crawled onto your Heavenly Father's lap for no other reason than to *enjoy* him, and you let him wrap his arms around you so he could *enjoy* you? You weren't trying to impress him with your accomplishments. All you wanted in those quiet moments was to treasure the fellowship with your Heavenly Father. God's tender, compassionate love toward his people is expressed in like manner throughout Scripture. One of my favorites was also written by David, "As a father has compassion on his children, so the LORD has compassion on those who fear Him." (Psalm 103:13, HCSB)

On the very day I wrote this chapter, God gave me a beautiful picture of his compassionate love. My wife Megan, who is a wonderful mom, was watching our three boys play in the backyard. At the time, our oldest was only four years old, so monitoring their movements is akin to herding cats. During a tiny window of opportunity when Megan was distracted, our two-year-old Marcus decided to leave our yard and explore the neighborhood. A dear lady a few houses away spotted him on the road, so she kindly took him by the hand and returned him to us. Megan was mortified when she looked up to see Marcus coming down our driveway accompanied by a stranger. Megan held her composure long enough to express her gratitude; then she went indoors and burst into tears.

I wonder, why did my wife cry? I know the obvious answer. Something terrible could have happened to Marcus. I get that. But what's the big deal? I mean really. Marcus contributes nothing tangible to our family. He's too young to get a job. He's too small to mow the lawn. He can't even bathe himself. The point is, he's not a very *useful* member of the family. Frankly, he's a lot of work. So why was Megan so happy to get him back?

Are you aghast at the cold, calculating way I speak of my children? If so, your moral compass is in good working order. You understand that family love is so much more than how useful someone is to the family. It is a deeply emotional love, with the parent's heartstrings wrapped all around the child. Because we are created in God's image, that parental love has been stamped into our hearts by our Heavenly Father. Our love for our children reflects his love for us.

Why then do some of us view God's love as purely a practical thing, that it's all about our usefulness to him? What a terrible distortion of who God is. God is wonderfully warm and affectionate toward his children. "You have **not** received a spirit that makes you **fearful slaves**," writes Paul to his Christian family. "Instead, you received God's Spirit when he adopted you as **his own children**. Now we call him, 'Abba, Father.' For his Spirit joins with our spirit to affirm that we are God's children." (Romans 8:15–16, NLT)

Paul expresses it perfectly. We who have placed our faith in Jesus Christ have become *children* of our Heavenly Father rather than mere *slaves* in his household. Slaves are brought into a household for one reason—to work. Slaves are property, tools to be used. But that is not our identity in Christ. Through the death and resurrection of Jesus Christ, God has adopted us into his family and made us his *children*. Again, not *slaves* but *children*. In fact, the Holy Spirit stirs within us, leading us to cry out and call God *Abba*, or "Daddy."

Whether you view yourself as a slave or a child makes all the difference in the world. I remember clearly the time God showed me the distinction in a way that touched me deeply. Before I share what happened, though, I need to tell you a little more of my story.

I served as a pastor for over a dozen years in northwestern Pennsylvania. I entered pastoral ministry when I was young because God had lit a fire in my heart to teach the Bible. At the time, it just seemed obvious I should become a pastor. Once I landed in pastoral ministry, however, I realized the work entailed a lot more than sitting in my office writing sermons all day.

The work of a pastor, contrary to what I imagined, involves very public, people-intensive responsibilities. Unfortunately, my introspective personality was not a good fit for the role. The congregations I served were wonderful, but the work kept me emotionally exhausted. Thus, I found myself in a demoralizing predicament: I was serving in a way I *thought* God wanted me to serve, but I was thoroughly miserable doing it.

The day finally arrived when I realized I had to make a change, for my own sanity as well as Megan's. So, I did the unthinkable: I left pastoral ministry and became just an average person again. As you might expect, the decision was personally devastating. I was convinced I had let God down. I had abandoned my call. And all my friends who were impressed that I was called by God to be a pastor were left wondering what in the world happened. How could the Lord view me as anything but a massive disappointment?

In retrospect, I can say with confidence that God's hand was at work the whole time. He knew what was best for me, and, out of compassion, he was leading me to a better place. I often tell people, "God answered more prayers to get me out of pastoral ministry than he did to get me in." That's no joke. Although my whole life seemed adrift, my Heavenly Father was preparing me for a new and better season of serving Him—and loving Him.

The process of transitioning from pastor to civilian, however, was agonizing. I became so depressed over my lot in life, Megan urged me to see a Christian counselor. Finally, I did, out of desperation. At my first appointment, something remarkable happened. To get the session started, the counselor asked about my family life growing up. As I began to talk about my dad, who had recently passed away, I suddenly burst into tears. I was shocked by my own breakdown. I never saw it coming. I had no idea so much of my internal turmoil had anything to do with my father. That moment became a turning point. Finally, my heart lay open so God could begin his work of mending the deep, deep hurts I had been carrying all my life. Little did I know how much my relationship with my dad had affected how I viewed my Heavenly Father.

I loved my dad. And my dad loved me. But we had no idea how to convey it to one another. We were complete opposites: He was a man's man, a man of action, thick-skinned, forceful with his opinions, and fearless in confronting others. Now convert every one of those attributes to its opposite, and you have a pretty good idea who I was as a kid: timid by nature, a thinker more than a doer, and with a tender heart that bruised easily.

As I grew older, conversations with Dad became harder. As soon as we discussed the weather and the local sports teams, we ran out of things to talk about. We'd sit at the same dinner table with a vast ocean between us, and neither of us knew how to cross to other side. We loved each other. We respected each other. But we could not *connect*.

I now realize, after years of struggling, how I carried all that baggage into my relationship with my Heavenly Father. My Heavenly Father was simply a cosmic-sized version of my dad. He was there. I knew he loved me. (He told me so in the Bible.) But he felt far away. I never *connected* with him.

But God is not content with a long-distance relationship with his children. He wants to connect on the heart-level. Recall Paul's words: "You received God's Spirit when he adopted you as his own children. Now we call him 'Abba, Father ...'" The Aramaic word *Abba* may have been a nursery word in Jesus' day, that is, an intimate way a baby calls out to his dad. Do you hear the ring of familiarity? Momma, Dadda, *Abba*. It's the longing in our hearts, inspired by the Holy Spirit, to reach our arms toward Heaven and cry, *"Abba!"*

As I sit in our basement composing this manuscript, there are days I hear our little Marcus upstairs babbling one of the few words he knows: "Dadda, Dadda, Dadda..." He wants to know, *Dad, when are you coming up to see me?* His heart has a natural longing for daddy. And as God's children, we have that longing too: "For [God's] Spirit joins with our spirit to affirm that we are God's children." Do you feel that ache in your heart to be close to your Heavenly Father? Do you feel his Spirit wooing you to his embrace?

Many years ago, during a visit to my parents' house, I smuggled out some old family movies recorded on 8mm film and had them converted to VHS tapes. (They are already obsolete. Now I need to transfer them to DVD.) What a trip down memory lane, to pop in the cassette and watch those old movies. One scene remains fresh in my memory: My dad, incredibly young at the time, was lying on the couch and holding me high when I was an infant. I could see the pleasure in his eyes. My dad loved me. He delighted in me.

Discovering that old movie was a happy-sad moment. I could tell, yes, my dad loved me after all. But it saddened me to realize how much of that unguarded affection we lost over the years. I don't blame my dad. I believe he loved me the best he knew how. Really, there's more reason to rejoice than to be sad because I now have in my mind a winsome image of my Heavenly Father's love for me: Happy, delighted, holding me high. He says, "I love you." And in my limited vocabulary, I reply, *"Abba."* Daddy.

A Long Walk Spoiled

Yes, God invites us to enjoy a child-father relationship with him, where his affectionate love washes away our shame and fear. But here's the problem: Many of us struggle to believe such a relationship is possible. Why is that? Why are we hesitant to accept what God offers so freely? The reasons are as old as mankind, dating back all the way to the Garden of Eden.

Consider the personal friendship Adam and Eve enjoyed with God while living in the garden, before their fall into sin. It was nothing unusual for them to go on long walks with their wonderful creator as suggested in this tantalizing verse, "Then the man and his wife heard the sound of the Lᴏʀᴅ God walking in the garden at the time of the evening breeze." (Genesis 3:8, HCSB) Think of it. When we say Adam and Eve walked with God, it's no theological metaphor. Adam and Eve literally walked with him side by side when he visited their neighborhood!

It's fascinating to trace through Scripture how the word "walk" became a vivid word-picture to describe a godly life. Early in Genesis, we find this mysterious biography: "***Enoch walked with God;*** then he was not there because God took him." (Genesis 5:24, HCSB) To me, the term "walk" speaks of relationship. Personally, I only go on walks with people I am very close to, such as my wife, my kids, or a good friend. Enoch, it seems, sought God's companionship, he wanted to stay by God's side, he wanted to go wherever God went. Enoch's love for the Lord went beyond simply *doing* things for him; it's also about *being with him*. Obedience, yes, but also relationship.

This provides fresh insight into Micah's summary of the godly life which we read earlier, "O people, the Lᴏʀᴅ has told you what is good, and this is what he requires of you: to do what is right, to love mercy, ***and to walk humbly with your God.***" (Micah 6:8, NLT.) When people cried out, "What do you require of us, Lord?", he extended an invitation: "Come, let us walk together." It's a stirring picture of relationship, conjuring idyllic memories of the Garden of Eden.

Let's be honest, though. Those long walks with the Lord changed radically once Adam and Eve were booted from paradise. They no longer rushed to the Lord's side when he visited. Instead, they burned with shame, aware of their nakedness. They attempted to cover themselves with meager garments made of fig leaves, a frantic attempt to hide from one another and, most of all, to hide from the unbearable holiness of God.

The trend continues today. We are desperate for something (*anything!*) to hide behind, to cover up all the stuff in our lives which brings us shame. While Adam knitted together some fig leaves, we knit together a patchwork of manmade accomplishments we hope is sufficient to cover our shortcomings. Without these fig leaves, we feel exposed. As an example, consider how we talk about prayer. "So how long should I pray each day? Is five minutes enough? Ten? I know some people who pray for thirty minutes."

How long should I pray?

What's my obligation?

What's God expecting?

What will make him happy?

How did it come to this? The living God who created the universe, the one who holds the answers to all mysteries, the one whose awesome presence drives angels to their knees—this God has invited us to come boldly into his throne room and enjoy the privilege of intimate friendship, and all we can do is look at the clock!? We find ourselves stuck, unable to simply enjoy the Lord's goodness because we cannot move beyond the nagging question, "Have I done enough?"

I wonder, is it possible we are still living in the shadow of the Law of Moses? Think about it. Under the Law, access to God was severely limited. God's presence was hidden behind a curtain in the temple, isolated to a small room called the Holy of Holies. Only the high priest could enter there, and once a year at that. The normal guy had no hope of getting so close to the Lord. The rest of us were left standing in the courtyard from a safe distance.

All those sacrifices and rituals under the Law communicated a vital truth: God is holy. Man is sinful. Distance must be maintained. Blood must be spilled to approach the Lord. All the ceremonies, again, were living prophecies pointing to Jesus Christ whose blood, at last, allows us to draw near to the Lord. In fact, the moment Jesus Christ surrendered his spirit on the cross, the huge curtain in the temple, which separated man from God, was suddenly torn in two, ripped from top to bottom, a clear sign this was an act of God (Matthew 27:51). God had sent the world a powerful message: The blood of his son has opened the way into the presence of the Lord. No more sacrifices are needed. The ultimate sacrifice has been made. God has been satisfied!

In celebration of this amazing development, Paul writes, "Because of Christ and our faith in him, we can now come boldly and confidently into God's presence." (Ephesians 3:12, NLT) *Boldly and confidently*, the very opposite of approaching him with shame and hesitation. If Christ is your savior, God's invitation to you is unmistakable: "Come to me boldly! Come to me confidently!"

So, let me ask you again: Have you learned to delight in the Lord's love? Or are you still sewing fig leaves together? In his presence do you feel welcomed or do you feel exposed? Have you felt the joy of your Father's delight? Or do you imagine him glowering over you, asking, "What have you done for me lately?"

Would it surprise you to learn that God enjoys his friendship with you, that he enjoys taking walks with you simply because his relationship with you gives him pleasure? Yes, your Heavenly Father wants to be with you, not only to walk with you but to dine with you. Jesus himself expressed the invitation this way: "Look! I stand at the door and knock. If you hear my voice and open the door, I will come in, and we will share a meal together as friends." (Revelation 3:20, NLT)

There's a startling parallel between the opening chapters of Genesis and the closing chapters of Revelation. Early in Genesis, we find paradise, the Garden of Eden, a place of breathtaking beauty, a place where we can enjoy long, unhurried walks with our creator.

There we enjoy God's friendship. Of course, in Genesis chapter three, we are exiled from Eden. And now there is distance between God and mankind which will only grow deeper as the centuries pass.

Let us now leap ahead. Fan through all the pages of your Bible, crossing millennia of history in mere seconds, until you come to the end of the age, the last two chapters of Revelation. There we find in God's eternal kingdom that Eden has been restored. The Tree of Life has returned (22:2). Have you ever viewed the Bible that way? The first two chapters: The paradise that was lost. The last two chapters: Paradise restored, forever.

There's a fascinating detail in Revelation 21. As God ushers in paradise forevermore, he shouts a message at the top of his lungs. "Look, God's home is now among his people! He will live with them, and they will be his people. God himself will be with them." (Revelation 21:3, NLT)

Four different ways, in that one verse, God repeats the same truth: God and his people are living together again. He shouts it, and he repeats it. Apparently, this momentous restoration means a great deal to our Heavenly Father, as if he has been looking forward to this reunion a long, long time. He's the tenderhearted father who looks up and sees in the distance that his prodigal children are finally coming home. The celebration is about to begin.

Maybe that's what history has been about all along, God doing the hard work of getting us from the opening chapters of Genesis to the closing chapters of Revelation. All those millennia of sweat, blood, and toil were the long journey back to the garden. And in the center of it all, like a stake driven through the heart of history, stands the cross of Jesus Christ. All of that so the Lord could shout with thunderous joy, "God's home is now among his people!"

Maybe our Heavenly Father has missed those long walks together as much as we have.

Chapter 5

Love Unashamed

A s our Heavenly Father's love floods our hearts, we understand why John the apostle was so excited to proclaim, "See how very much our Father loves us, for he calls us his children, and that is what we are!" (1 John 3:1, NLT) God never intended for us to store this love on ice as mere theological trivia. He wants it to rouse our hearts and stir our emotions, so much so it causes us to sing and dance with joy. If all that sounds a little over-the-top, allow me to introduce you to Psalm 149. Brace yourself. Things get a little rowdy:

> Let Israel *celebrate* its Maker;
> let the children of Zion *rejoice* in their King.
> Let them *praise* His name with *dancing*
> and *make music to Him* with tambourine and lyre.
>
> (Psalm 149:2-3, HCSB)

The psalmist is effervescent with elation. He rejoices, he is glad, he praises, he dances, and he makes music. Now, read one verse further to find out why the psalmist is so giddy. "For Yahweh [the LORD] takes pleasure in His people." (v.4) The psalmist is overcome with rollicking joy because—miracle of miracles—Almighty God takes pleasure (delights!) in his people. God *enjoys* his people. In fact, the psalmist is so bursting with emotion, he can hardly sleep at night: "Let the godly celebrate in triumphal glory; let them shout for joy on their beds." (v.5)

It's the joy of a teenage girl, the school wallflower, who has just been asked to the prom by her secret crush, the handsome varsity quarterback. *Why in the world did you choose me?! What do you see in me?!* To her amazement, she sees delight sparkling in his eyes. *I don't believe it! He really wants to be with me*—Can you believe it? God wants to be with you.

Is it possible that behind all your striving to do something *huge* for God is a desire to win the heart of your Heavenly Father? Here's the irony: You already have what you're working so hard to acquire. Your Father's heartstrings are wrapped all around you. He knows your name. Your picture is in his wallet. He has affection for you. God delights in you. He even bursts into singing:

> The LORD your God is living among you.
> He is a mighty savior.
> He will take delight in you with gladness.
> With his love, he will calm all your fears.
> He will rejoice over you with joyful songs.

(Zephaniah 3:17, NLT)

When I read passages like that, I realize I cannot overstate the love God has for his children. No wonder Paul was zealous for his brothers and sisters in Christ to experience, deep in their hearts, God's love to the fullest (Ephesians 3:14-19). His love is transformational. Like breakers at the ocean shore, his love washes over us again and again and again, cleansing away shame and replenishing our souls with joy.

Think back to my *Abba, Father* story a few pages ago, how my imperfect relationship with my dad became the lens through which I viewed God's love. There we find an important lesson: The primary relationships in our lives tend to shape how we express and receive love. It's no coincidence, then, that the very questions I harbored about my dad, I also harbored about God: *Do I measure up to your expectations? Are you ashamed of me? Have I let you down somehow? What do you want from me?*

Many brothers and sisters in Christ, I'm convinced, are dogged by such questions. As a result, shame rather than joy prevails in their relationship with their Heavenly Father. If that's where you are, read carefully a verse I discovered years ago which transformed my view of God: "Jesus and the ones he makes holy have the same Father. That is why Jesus is not ashamed to call them his brothers and sisters." (Hebrews 2:11, NLT)

Did you see it? Jesus is *not ashamed* to call you his brother or his sister. When you walk into the room, he doesn't turn away. He doesn't avert his eyes. He doesn't look at his watch and find an excuse to leave. On the contrary, Jesus welcomes you with a smile into his presence. He is so glad you came. He embraces you. You see affection in his eyes. He treasures you with a love beyond measure. Here is the one place you find full acceptance.

When I was a kid, we sang a rousing song in Vacation Bible School with this line, "His banner over me is love." Only years later did I learn the phrase came from the Bible. (Imagine that!) The stanza comes from the Song of Solomon, a beautiful Hebrew poem extolling the romance, love, and sensuality between a man and his bride, all expressed in good taste. The book also serves as a picture of Jesus' love for his church. If that interpretation surprises you, keep in mind that all through the Bible, God compares his love for his people to a groom's love for his bride (Isaiah 54:5).

So, the poetic phrase, "His banner over me is love," comes from the lips of the blushing bride in the Song of Solomon. As the handsome groom escorts her to the banquet hall for a celebratory feast, she proclaims with joy, "He has brought me to his banquet hall, and his banner over me is love." (2:4, NASB) In a public display of affection, the groom holds a banner over his bride, and on the banner is printed "LOVE." Of course, this is poetry. I doubt he carried an actual banner. It's the language of emotion, written to portray a heart-stirring truth. But what truth?

The imagery puzzled me for a long time until, one day, I felt its full meaning when I discovered how the New Living Translation rendered that same verse: "He brings me to the banquet hall, so everyone can see how much he loves me." (NLT, 1996 ed.) What a picture of the groom's enthusiastic love for his bride—even better, what an image of God's whole-hearted love for his people. Jesus, your groom, is excited to show you off to his friends. I don't know about you, but I need to hear that, a lot. And I don't think I'm alone.

Recently I was with a group of Christian men discussing the challenges of being godly fathers. One of the older men named Dave, whose kids are now grown and walking with the Lord, related a story which still brings tears to his eyes. Years ago, the company he worked for hosted a bring-your-son-to-work day, so he invited his young son Brian to the plant and gave him the royal tour. At one point, filled with a father's pride, Dave put his arm around Brian's shoulders as they walked down a long corridor. They approached the open doorway to a room where several electricians were working, and Dave, in a flash of embarrassment, pulled his arm away from his son.

Even after all these years, Dave grieves when he recalls the moment he faltered as a young dad, unwilling to let others see the affection he had for his child. How many of us can relate to Dave's struggle to show affection? More to the point, how many of us identify with his son Brian? Can you recall a day someone you loved pulled his hand away? You were left wondering: *Are you ashamed of me? Is there something about me that embarrasses you?*

Here's the good news: Jesus is not ashamed to pour his affection on you. He takes you to the banquet hall to celebrate with his friends, and when all those eyes turn to stare, he does not pull his arm away. He squeezes you even tighter, holding you warmly against his bosom. His banner over you is love. And he's there so everyone can see just how much he loves you.

What Love Can Do

I know what some of you are thinking. You worry where this lavish emphasis on God's love might lead. Am I enticing you to settle for a passive Christian life, where we gaze at our navels and reflect on the wonders of God's love? Do we risk losing the motivation to serve him?

A couple thoughts: First, I assume you have some idea what this book is about, if for no other reason than you read the summary on the back cover. If the topic piqued your interest and you've made it this far, chances are you're already wired to serve the Lord. I doubt your problem is ambition. You have that in spades. Your struggle is overcoming anxiety about your performance: *Am I doing the Lord's will? Have I done enough? Is he pleased with me?* You don't need me to crack the whip and tell you to try harder. You've done that to yourself for some time now.

Second, a genuine, heart-level understanding of God's love does not lead to passivity. It leads to passion—joyful passion. You make the transition from guilt-driven service to joy-filled service. As Nehemiah proclaimed, "The joy of the Lord is your strength." (Nehemiah 8:10, NASB) To prove the point, allow me to introduce you to a man whose name is familiar to us all: Simon Peter, preeminent leader of Jesus' twelve disciples. He learned firsthand the transformative power of Jesus' love.

If you know anything about Peter, you know the Gospels portray him as outspoken and ambitious for the Lord, often to a fault. In the upper room, on the very night Jesus was betrayed, Peter's ambition was on full display. After Jesus warned his disciples they would all abandon him once he was arrested, Peter drew a line in the sand and declared, "Even if everyone runs away, I will certainly not!" (Mark 14:29, HCSB) Jesus, who knew better, broke the news that Peter would disown him three times before the rooster crowed the next morning. Unfazed, Peter only doubled down: "If I have to die with You, I will never deny You!" (v.31)

Much of Peter's avowed dedication, we'll soon discover, was for public consumption. The Gospels record how he folded like a cheap tent once he came under pressure. He overpromised and under-delivered. How do we explain it? Was Peter at heart a dishonest man? I don't think so. I believe he was merely prone to the same polluted ambitions we all struggle with. Peter, it seems, had something to prove, not only to his friends but also to the Lord.

When it comes to ambition for the Lord, our hearts are murky vessels. There is a subtle but profound difference between wanting to *please* the Lord and wanting to *prove* ourselves to the Lord. Often lurking behind the latter is the drive to achieve celebrity status in the kingdom of God. Celebrity status does not require worldwide fame or notoriety. It simply requires that in my circle of Christian friends, I am the spiritual guy everyone else admires.

In many churches, you can rocket to stardom just by declaring your intention to enter vocational ministry: Commit to the mission field or commit to becoming a pastor. From that day forward, all your friends will speak of you in reverent tones. And you imagine the Lord is pretty impressed with you as well. Do not underestimate the allure of being a celebrity, even within a small group of friends. Peter was that guy. When Jesus gave the altar call, Peter went forward with the kind of zeal that makes everyone else feel ashamed for holding back. And Peter would bask in his celebrity status—for a little while.

That same evening, the local religious leaders arrested Jesus and took him to the courtyard of Caiaphas the high priest for a mock trial, what would prove to be history's worst miscarriage of justice. To Peter's credit, he followed Jesus right into the courtyard despite the dangers, even after most of his friends had run away.

But Peter's crash to earth soon followed. A mere servant girl asked if he was one of Jesus' followers, and Peter's resolve crumbled immediately. He flat-out lied, denying he knew Jesus. After the girl inquired again, Peter repeated the lie. The conversation stirred the interest of the crowd, and soon others began to inquire. The tension escalated until Peter caved completely.

> But Peter said, "Man, I don't know what you're talking about!" Immediately, while he was still speaking, a rooster crowed. Then the Lord turned and looked at Peter. So Peter remembered the word of the Lord, how He had said to him, "Before the rooster crows today, you will deny Me three times." And he went outside and wept bitterly.
>
> (Luke 22:60-62, HCSB)

For me, the most heartbreaking moment is when Jesus, after the third denial, turns and looks Peter in the eye. No words are spoken. No words are necessary. In that awful moment, when Peter realizes he has betrayed his Lord and friend, his heart shatters. Its ugly contents spill out for the whole world to see: his selfish ambition, his fragile resolve, and his cowardice. In the end, all that spiritual bravado proved to be a weak façade.

Broken and humiliated, Peter runs away and weeps bitterly. It's the soul-wrenching grief of a servant who has disappointed the Lord he loves, a servant whose life has become an embarrassment. That's a hard pill to swallow for a man who prides himself in his dedication to the kingdom. But all that internal baggage had to be destroyed so the Lord could perform a major renovation in Peter's heart.

Now, let's leap ahead in the gospel narrative. Just as he promised, Jesus has risen from the tomb and appeared to his disciples. At first confused and fearful, they finally embrace the good news: Jesus Christ their Lord, savior, and friend has conquered the grave. He is alive!

Despite the elation of those post-resurrection days, you can imagine the dark cloud hovering over Peter. The memories of his public failure are still raw. Whenever the disciples are gathered, everyone senses the elephant in the room: Big-man Peter crashed and burned a few nights ago. Peter's manner is now subdued. Gone is all the bravado. He has learned what he's really made of, and he's humiliated by it.

One day, out of the blue, comes the moment Peter has dreaded, when Jesus confronts the elephant in the room. It had to happen. Jesus does not settle for surface-level transformation. He is all about shining his light into our dark and hidden places so he can enter in. He is all about truth, but truth carried in the arms of perfect love. The account is recorded in John 21:15-19.

Here is how it happened. One morning, Jesus cooked up breakfast on the beach for his disciples, a humble act of hospitality by the king who was only days away from assuming his throne in glory. By the time the meal was over, I imagine Peter was issuing a sigh of relief because no one brought up the awkward topic of his public meltdown. Then all of a sudden, he hears Jesus kindly call him by his original name, the one given by his parents, "Simon son of John ...."

Peter cringes. Oh, no. Here it comes.

"Simon son of John," says Jesus, "Do you love me more than these?"

Oh, what a painful question! Jesus is sticking his finger right in the open wound. He is essentially saying, Peter, just a few nights ago, you boasted how your devotion exceeded that of all the other disciples. I give you the opportunity to boast once more. Do you still claim to love me more than your friends do? But Peter is all done with boasting. No longer willing to compare himself to anyone else, he simply replies, "Yes, Lord, you know that I love you." No boasting. No comparisons. Just a soft-spoken admission of love.

There's something subtle going on in Peter's reply which is evident in the original Greek. Peter uses a different word for love than Jesus did. Jesus used the Greek verb *agapao* (ah-gah-PAH-oh). We often refer to this kind of love in its noun form: *Agape* (ah-GAH-pay). *Agape* love denotes selfless commitment regardless of the consequences. When your enemy slaps you and you turn the other cheek, that's *agape* love. When you show commitment to your spouse when he or she least deserves it, that's *agape* love.

Peter, though, is unwilling even to speak the word for selfless love. He settles for a word that denotes loving affection, the mutual fondness between friends or between members of a family. It's the verb *phileo.* (phil-LEH-oh). We might paraphrase his answer to Jesus this way, "Yes, Lord, you know you have my loving affection." Loving affection, that's the best Peter can offer.

In reply, Jesus says, "Feed my lambs." Jesus will need someone to shepherd his newborn church after he ascends to heaven. Jesus offers the position of chief shepherd to Peter. I surmise this was the last thing Peter expected. Perhaps he was waiting for the severe rebuke, another "Get behind me, Satan!"

Peter is still coming to terms with what he heard when Jesus asks him a second time, "Simon son of John, do you love me?" Jesus has scaled back the question this time. He does not ask Peter to compare his love to anyone else. He only seeks a confession of love. But he still employs the word *agapao*, the love of highest commitment.

Hurt and confused, Peter wonders what is behind this inquisition. Again, he replies, "Yes, Lord, you know you have my loving affection." Peter has come to terms with his frailties all too well. He will not presume to speak the word for selfless love. Affection and friendship are the best he can offer. *Lord, maybe you should find someone else to lead your church—someone made of better stuff than I am.*

Here comes Jesus' reply, "Take care of my sheep."

What!? Lord, didn't you hear what I said? My love is imperfect! I faltered when you needed me most! I have nothing to offer you! I am NOTHING, Lord! I am NOTHING!

To Peter's dismay, Jesus comes at him a third time, "Simon son of John, do I have your loving affection?" In my paraphrase, I bring out what is hidden in the Greek. Jesus now uses the word for love that Peter uses, *phileo*. Jesus lowers himself, as it were, to Peter's level. *Peter, your loving affection is good enough. I accept what you have to give.*

In complete agony now, Peter pours out his heartache, "Lord, you know all things; you know you have my loving affection."

Again Jesus replies, "Feed my sheep." Yes, Peter has a job to do. And Jesus goes on to explain what it will cost Peter in the years ahead, how the responsibility will require great sacrifice.

Only with time and distance will Peter fully appreciate what the Lord did for him that morning. Peter, just days before, had denied his Lord three times. By allowing Peter to confess his love three times, Jesus drew Peter back into the fold and put behind him that terrible failure. And Jesus chose to have this conversation in front of the other disciples so everyone could witness Peter's restoration. What a beautiful embodiment of our Lord's amazing grace.

Most important of all, Peter learned something priceless: The beauty of the Christian life has nothing to do with our love and ambition for the Lord. It has everything to do with the Lord's love for us. Please don't miss this truth.

The real beauty of our relationship with Christ
Is not our love for him
But his love for us.

For me, that conversation on the beach between Peter and Jesus is one of the most poignant in all of Scripture because I easily picture myself in Peter's sandals. Early in my Christian life, I had grand visions of all I would accomplish for the Lord. I hate to admit it, but I was buzz-drunk on the prospect of being a local celebrity in the kingdom. People were impressed by my spiritual stature, my giftedness, and my Biblical knowledge—and I enjoyed the attention. But God let me run headlong under my own steam until I outran my meager abilities, and then I crashed. My Heavenly Father let me crash, knowing all along what was best for me. I needed to see what weak stuff I was made of.

I needed to stop proving myself to everyone.

I needed to stop proving myself to God.

I needed, finally, to get over myself.

Above all, I needed to open myself up to the vast ocean-depths of God's love. Really, isn't that what it's all about? "This is real love— not that we loved God, but that he loved us and sent his Son as a sacrifice to take away our sins." (1 John 4:10, NLT) Again,

The real beauty of our relationship with Christ
Is not our love for him
But his love for us.

Are you still worried this emphasis on God's love will take the edge off your service? After Peter's meltdown and restoration, once he had gotten over himself and experienced the Lord's loving affection, something amazing happened. Gratitude became the rocket fuel for Peter's ambition. His newfound joy carried him through decades of faithful service. He stayed faithful to the very end, even to the point of death on a cross, all because of his devotion to the Lord Jesus Christ. That's commitment.

In his early days, Peter's pride and ambition failed him. The love and kindness of Jesus restored him. Then Peter rose from the ashes of failure, brimming with gratitude, to serve the Lord faithfully the rest of his life. And he finished well. He finished very well. That's what love can do.

Remember, it's not about how much you love the Lord.

It's all about how much he loves you.

Stop trying to impress him.

Stop trying to prove yourself.

Let him love you.

Just let him love you.

And be amazed at what his love can do.

Part 3
Gratitude: Gateway to Glory

Be thankful in all circumstances,
for this is God's will for you who belong to Christ Jesus.

-1 Thessalonians 5:18
(NLT)

Chapter 6

The Glory of Gratitude

Adeep, abiding love for God springs from the realization how much he first loved us and continues to love us still. His love is relentless as it is compassionate. Our service for him, then, is not an attempt to impress him nor win his affection. Our service springs from gratitude—heartfelt gratitude for the Lord's wonderful kindness.

In fact, praise and gratitude are central to our calling as Christians. "You are a chosen race," writes the apostle Peter, "a royal priesthood, a holy nation, a people for His possession, *so that you may proclaim the praises* of the One who called you out of darkness into His marvelous light." (1 Peter 2:9, HCSB) Be sure to read and reread Peter's words until you see it clearly: God rescued us from darkness so that we might declare his praises. Peter's voice is not alone, as Paul strikes a similar chord: *"Be thankful in all circumstances*, for this is God's will for you who belong to Christ Jesus." (1 Thessalonians 5:18, NLT)

We now turn our hearts to the topics of praise and thanksgiving, and this marks a major transition in *The Glorious Ordinary.* From this point forward, you will find down-to-earth advice on how to transform the humdrum moments of your day into glorious events. In this chapter, you'll discover how genuine gratitude to God, expressed through praise, serves as a gateway to entering the sacred.

A Short Step to Glory

Watch closely. Something amazing is about to happen. Imagine a very ordinary scene in a very ordinary home. It's dinner time. Mom, dad, and the kids have gathered around the kitchen table. Tonight's meal: fried chicken, green beans, and tossed salad. Dad hushes the animated chatter until everyone grows quiet. Heads bow. Eyes close. And dad offers his thanks to the Lord for the meal. After the "Amen," everyone reaches for the nearest dish.

Did you catch it? Can you identify the moment this normal meal became a glorious event? Here's the key: As soon as dad offered his prayer, the family mealtime became something sacred in God's eyes. Yes, sacred, as Paul the apostle makes clear: "For everything created by God is good, and nothing should be rejected if it is received with thanksgiving, *since it is sanctified by the word of God and by prayer.*" (1 Timothy 4:4-5, HCSB)

Please don't miss Paul's meaning: When we say "Thank you" to the Lord at the supper table, our prayer sanctifies the mealtime. Again, *sanctifies.* It has crossed the line from the secular to the holy. To put it another way, the meal has been dedicated to a special, divine purpose, all because dad gave thanks to God. Did you have any idea that saying grace was such a big deal?

So, why does God bestow such importance on a simple mealtime prayer? We find the answer in the immediate context of what Paul wrote. He was correcting a perverse kind of spirituality that misguided teachers had introduced to the Ephesian church, namely, that if you want to be truly spiritual, you must deny yourself earthly pleasures like food and marriage (4:3). That kind of insidious teaching, Paul warned, has its source in the demonic (4:1).

You see, God by nature is compassionate and generous. He enjoys blessing his people with good things. Paul mentions two such blessings in context: marriage and food. God welcomes us to enjoy these gifts with gratitude. The Devil, on the other hand, tempts us to view them with disdain because it's his ambition to rob God of praise. That's why expressing our gratitude to God, even in the most ordinary way, is a cosmic event. Heaven shouts for joy because finally (finally!) someone has given God the credit he deserves.

It's true: A simple, heartfelt prayer over a meal transforms the ordinary into the sacred. The mealtime becomes an act of worship where we acknowledge the Lord's kindness and generosity. Now imagine what happens when our gratitude overflows the dinner table and pours into every corner of our lives. Praise will transform any moment, even the most ordinary, into a sacred event. In fact, we are about to discover that a lifestyle of genuine gratitude brings more pleasure to the Lord than many of the big and impressive sacrifices we strive to bring him.

Memo from Heaven

Three thousand years ago, God sent a memo to his people, the nation of Israel. The message, found in Psalm 50, discloses something about God's heart many will find surprising.

> I have no complaint about your sacrifices
>   or the burnt offerings you constantly offer.
> But I do not need the bulls from your barns
>   or the goats from your pens.
> For all the animals of the forest are mine,
>   and I own the cattle on a thousand hills.
>
> (Psalm 50: 8-10, NLT)

Notice how God had "no complaint" about Israel's compliance with all the rituals required by the Law of Moses. Oddly enough, however, the sacrifices left him unsatisfied. Something was missing, and a few verses later, the Lord discloses what he desired above all: ***"Make thankfulness your sacrifice to God***, and keep the vows you made to the Most High." (v.14) To put it another way, God longed for a people who expressed gratitude to him and who kept their promises. King David echoes a similar theme in Psalm 69:

> I will praise God's name with singing,
>   and I will honor him with thanksgiving.
> For this will please the Lord more than sacrificing cattle,
>   more than presenting a bull with its horns and hooves.

(Psalm 69: 30-31, NLT)

Again, God prefers praise over sacrifice. Honestly, I find these Psalms astonishing because the Jewish Bible (our Old Testament) commanded those ritual sacrifices. But God longed for more. He longed for gratitude among his people. So, why does God value gratitude so highly? Perhaps we can gain some insight by returning, once again, to that spiritual laboratory called marriage—my own marriage to be exact.

When the Christmas season approaches, my wife Megan and I will sometimes discuss our expectations regarding gifts for each other. In the interests of being thrifty, we'll agree on a modest dollar-limit. It's a fine tradition but one that is seriously flawed for one reason: I typically ignore the agreement and end up spending way more than I promised.

I wish I could tell you that my selfless love for Megan wholly inspires my generosity. Truthfully, I suspect much of my extravagance springs from pride and insecurity. Yes, there's an element of pride. When I unwrap the gift Megan bought for me, purchased within our approved budget, and then she unwraps the expensive smartphone I bought for her, I feel pretty good about myself. Megan lights up with surprise. Friends and family are impressed. And I delight in knowing I purchased the "Oh, wow!" gift that got everyone talking.

And then there's the element of insecurity. The big "Oh, wow!" gift is my attempt to compensate for all the times I failed to appreciate my wife as I should. The days are too many to count when Megan shows amazing patience with our kids, goes above and beyond the call of duty as a mom, is thoughtful in ways that leave me humbled—and I neglect to express the appreciation she deserves. So, at Christmastime, I lay a whole bunch of money on the altar to make up for my negligence.

But here's the thing. Megan has kindly reminded me over the years that big gifts aren't necessary. Rather, the small, daily expressions of affection are what mean a great deal to her: the hug in the kitchen, the kisses throughout the day, the words of encouragement, the romantic little notes– the list goes on. I must confess, though, swiping my credit card at Walmart comes more naturally than wrapping my arms around my wife in a romantic embrace. Since we've been married, I've had to train myself, sometimes with great exertion, to show affection, the kind that is expressed every day with sincerity.

I see the same dynamic in our relationship with the Lord. Our Heavenly Father says to us, "I don't need the big and expensive gifts. (I own the cattle on a thousand hills after all! What could you possibly give me?) Here's what I really want: Genuine affection and gratitude expressed every day and with deep sincerity."

Is there a message here for those of us under pressure to accomplish something big for the Lord? Perhaps our Heavenly Father is saying, "Child, a genuine prayer of thanksgiving means more to me than all those sacrifices you've been stressing over. Why not set down your burdens, step into the sunshine, and offer up the sacrifice of praise?" It's really that simple. In Heaven's eyes, gratitude is a very big deal. And gratitude expressed through praise has a consecrating effect on the ordinary stuff of life.

Even though I find this truth woven throughout Scripture, it surprised me when I first discovered it. Perhaps you're feeling the same way. Maybe you're even a bit skeptical. If so, I have a suggestion: Let's take a long, hard look at the *opposite* of gratitude, that is, a negative, complaining spirit. The contrast, I believe, will help us understand why God receives so much pleasure from our praise.

Before we proceed, however, I should warn you: This brief study on *ingratitude* is unsettling as it is enlightening. Many of us will discover that our hearts require a major housecleaning to get rid of the ugly negativity festering there. But don't despair. Welcome the pain as God's loving invitation to a better way of living. Hear his words, embrace them as true, and choose the path that leads to glory. Remember, he loves you and has your best interests at heart.

Forgetting and Doubting

The spirit of negativity, so prevalent in the human heart, is the toxic byproduct of ingratitude and doubt. *Ingratitude* is willful-blindness to God's faithfulness in the past. And *doubt* refuses to trust him for the future. We see the ruinous effects of negativity in the world-famous case study forever preserved in Scripture: the tragic failure of the Exodus generation.

Those who've spent years attending Sunday school know the story well—how God raised up Moses to rescue the Israelites from slavery in Egypt and lead them to the Promised Land. Despite all the blessings God bestowed on that generation and despite all the miracles they witnessed, they soon entered a relentless spiral into negativity. They literally complained themselves to death. Psalm 106 provides a condensed history of their tragic decline.

> Our ancestors in Egypt
>> were not impressed by the Lord's miraculous deeds.
> **They soon forgot** his many acts of kindness to them.
>> Instead, they rebelled against him at the Red Sea.
> Even so, he saved them—
>> to defend the honor of his name
>> and to demonstrate his mighty power.
> He commanded the Red Sea to dry up.
> He led Israel across the sea as if it were a desert ...
> Then his people believed his promises.
> Then they sang his praise ...
>
> Yet how quickly they forgot what he had done!
> ... The people refused to enter the pleasant land,
>> for they wouldn't believe his promise to care for them.
> Instead, they **grumbled** in their tents
>> and refused to obey the Lord.
> Therefore, he solemnly swore
>> that he would kill them in the wilderness ...
>
> (Excerpts from Psalm 106, NLT)

The Exodus generation—who witnessed the ten plagues that ravaged Egypt, who experienced miraculous redemption from slavery, and who walked to freedom through the Red Sea—this same generation soon "forgot" what God had done for them. And "they wouldn't believe his promise to care for them." Instead they "grumbled" over their lot in life. It reads like a dark comedy.

We dare not laugh at this dark comedy, however, because many of us are prone to the same kind of negativity, which is why Paul urges us to heed the lessons of that generation: "Don't grumble as some of them did, and then were destroyed by the angel of death. These things happened to them as examples for us. They were written down to warn us who live at the end of the age." (1 Corinthians 10:10–11, NLT) If anyone thinks griping and complaining are minor sins, Paul's warning should lay that assumption to rest once and for all. (See, I told you this study would prove unsettling.)

It's tempting to downplay the severity of ingratitude because the world around us is awash in negativity. We just get used to all the griping. But God calls us upward to a better way, as expressed through Paul's words to the Philippian church, "Do everything without grumbling and arguing, so that you may be blameless and pure, children of God who are faultless in a crooked and perverted generation, among whom you shine like stars in the world." (Philippians 2:14–15, HCSB) Amazing, isn't it? When we remove "grumbling" and "arguing" from our lives, we "shine like stars in the world" in brilliant contrast to the dark negativity all around us.

Please don't miss it: People with a God-centered optimism bring glorious light to our world. Negative people bring darkness. In many and various ways, the Lord has pressed this truth into my heart.

After I left pastoral ministry, I worked for a small technology company for several years, and a Christian man named Bob managed our team of technicians. The opportunity for Christian fellowship on the job was priceless. We often prayed together, discussed the Bible, and kept each other encouraged in the Lord. One topic we frequently discussed was the importance of having a positive attitude in the workplace. Bob kindly brought the matter to my attention because, to be honest, I adopted a defeatist attitude whenever work became stressful. He reminded me, both as my boss and as a Christian brother, that negativity is contagious. It brings others down. At first,

I bristled at his reminders, but I soon realized God was using him to shape my character.

That lesson was reinforced over and over. When the time came to hire additional technicians, Bob asked me to join him when interviewing candidates. He told me that one quality to look for was a positive attitude. He knew from experience that one person's negativity can bring everyone else down. Boy, was he right. I witnessed firsthand how one bad apple can ruin the morale of a whole department, even an entire company. Badmouthing, griping, criticism, and pessimism— they spread like disease. That motivated me to take an honest look at my own conduct.

Indeed, Paul's metaphor of a star shining in the darkness is spot-on: A grateful-to-God spirit brightens our corner of the world, a truth very much in keeping with the theme of *The Glorious Ordinary.* We can achieve stardom in the kingdom of God by nurturing a hope-filled, thankful spirit.

Now, may I ask you a personal question? What do you bring to your corner of the world—the light of a God-centered optimism or the darkness of negativity? Do you bear the poisonous fruits of complaining? Bitterness? Destructive criticism? Moaning? Pessimism? Cynicism? Sarcasm? Or do you bring better things into people's lives, such as the delicious fruits of gratitude, hope, encouragement, and a godly optimism?

I invite you to reflect on the following verses, where we hear God calling us to a life filled with thanksgiving. If you're like me, they'll humble you as well as inspire you.

Be thankful in all circumstances,
for this is God's will for you who belong to Christ Jesus.
-1 Thessalonians 5:18, NLT

Obscene stories, foolish talk, and coarse jokes—these are not for you.
Instead, let there be thankfulness to God.

-Ephesians 5:4, NLT

And whatever you do, in word or in deed,
do everything in the name of the Lord Jesus,
giving thanks to God the Father through Him.

-Colossians 3:17, HCSB

Therefore, through Him let us continually offer up to God
a sacrifice of praise, that is, the fruit of our lips that confess His name.

-Hebrews 13:15, HCSB

Again, grateful praise invites heaven's glory, turning any moment into something sacred. Let's be honest, though. All this could devolve into a superficial exercise if we aren't careful, where we simply parrot the appropriate catchphrases throughout our day: "Praise the Lord!" "Thank you, Jesus!" Hollow clichés are hardly inspiring. Often they're annoying.

Surely, God is calling us to something much more profound. Our Heavenly Father enjoys praise that comes from a heart filled with *authentic* faith and *authentic* gratitude. The operative word is *authentic.* Authentic gratitude requires heart-level transformation, and that happens to be Jesus' specialty.

Jesus, the Great Optometrist

As I mentioned already, I had a deep streak of negativity for many years, but I didn't think much of it because, as far as I was concerned, my pessimism was rooted in a "realistic" view of the world. Christians who exuded a praise-the-Lord attitude were the ones out of touch, or so I assumed. Thanks to the Lord's leading, I realized my attitude had nothing to do with realism. It had everything to do with blindness. Like the Exodus generation, I was unable to see God's blessings right in front of me.

I began to suspect I had a vision-problem one day while reading Jesus' sermon on worry. The passage made little sense to me. Either Jesus' teaching was flawed (unlikely), or my faith was suffering from a serious blind spot (highly likely). Here are the verses that got me thinking:

> "Therefore I tell you, don't worry about your life, what you will eat; or about the body, what you will wear ... Consider the ravens: They don't sow or reap; they don't have a storeroom or a barn; yet God feeds them. Aren't you worth much more than the birds?
>
> "...Consider how the wildflowers grow: They don't labor or spin thread. Yet I tell you, not even Solomon in all his splendor was adorned like one of these! If that's how God clothes the grass, which is in the field today and is thrown into the furnace tomorrow, how much more will He do for you—you of little faith?"

(Jesus; Luke 12:22-28, HCSB)

For a long time, Jesus' sermon struck me as terribly Pollyannaish. *'Don't worry about your life? Just look at the pretty birds?' Who says stuff like that?!* Imagine a client getting that kind of advice from his investment advisor. "I'm concerned I don't have enough money saved for retirement," the client explains.

"Don't worry, you'll be fine," says the advisor with a glance toward his office window. "Look at the birds out there, how God provides for them. Aren't you more important than they are?"

"Um..."

"And look at the grassy field, how God clothes it with beautiful flowers."

Oh-KAY. The client stands up to leave. "Thank you for your time."

"Must you leave so soon?"

"I just remembered I have another appointment."

Had I been that client, I would have walked out, too. *This guy has a screw loose! I need to find a new financial advisor!* That's exactly how I felt about Jesus' teaching on faith and worry. I just didn't get it.

Then one day, the light came on. When Jesus looks at the world around him, he sees evidence of God's faithfulness—everywhere! He sees, not just a field full of birds, but evidence of his Heavenly Father's intimate involvement in the world, how he moves the levers of creation to feed the tiniest bird. And Jesus sees more than a flowery field. He sees a canvas where his Father has poured out his creativity—even though the field will be mowed down and fed to the cows by the end of the week. Now, if God cares for grass and birds with such attention to detail, how much more is he watching over us, his dear children?

Jesus' perspective reminds us that every moment of every day we have a choice: We can look for evidence of God's goodness, or we can settle for a God-less kind of pessimism. For example, when I walk through our house, I can choose to see a place in constant need of repair, walls that need painting, and dishes that need washing. Or I can look through the eyes of faith and see all the evidence of our Heavenly Father's kindness: He has given us a roof over our heads, a soft bed where we can sleep, and a furnace to keep us warm. How blessed we are.

I can gripe about the toys littering our house, or I can thank God for the sound of laughter from our three young boys. When I tackle a big challenge, I can imagine all the ways it could go wrong, or I can recall how, time and again, God has seen me through similar circumstances in the past. I can fixate on my shortcomings or thank the Lord for the gifts he's given me. I can dwell on the bleakness of my past or rejoice in the bright future I have in Christ Jesus.

So, how are you doing in this regard? When you consider your circumstances, are you prone to see lots of inspiration for praise or lots of reasons to complain? Those of you who have a deeply ingrained tendency toward negativity (like I did), all this sounds like a game of wishful thinking, doesn't it? If so, consider something else Jesus said: "The eye is the lamp of the body. If your eye is good, your whole body will be full of light. But if your eye is bad, your whole body will be full of darkness. So if the light within you is darkness—how deep is that darkness!" (Matthew 6:22-23, HCSB) The eye here represents how we see our circumstances and the world around us. Unhealthy eyes do not see the world from God's perspective, so darkness fills the body. And in darkness, all sorts of maladies thrive—hopelessness, despair, anger, bitterness, anxiety, and depression.

If you are struggling to find reasons to be thankful, then chances are your body is full of the very darkness Jesus warns about. Aren't you tired of living that way? What would you give to enjoy a full measure of optimism, joy, hope, peace, and confidence—a genuine heart-level transformation inspired by the Holy Spirit?

Think of it this way: If God has invited us to a lifestyle of thanksgiving, it only makes sense that our lives are filled with reasons to be grateful. If we're struggling to find those reasons, then our eyes are in poor health. Like the Exodus generation, we've become blind to God's blessings all around us. Somehow, we must train our eyes to see what's right in front of us.

And that brings us to the good news. Our poor vision doesn't have to be a terminal condition. With God's leading, we can learn to see again. It simply requires a heartfelt desire to change and a willingness to train. Yes, it requires training. "Train yourself in godliness," writes Paul. (1 Timothy 4:7, HCSB) And more to the point,

"Be transformed by the renewing of your mind." (Romans 12:2, HCSB).

Yes, we'll need to train our hearts and minds, but the payoff is huge. When the dam of negative thinking finally crumbles away, the Holy Spirit rushes into our hearts to deliver those heaven-sent blessings we've been longing for: real joy, real peace, and real gratitude. We'll begin to emanate authentic praise to the Lord. And those around us will be blessed by the light we bring. That's how you become one of God's brilliant stars shining in a very dark world.

Before we depart this chapter, I want to speak to those who have endured chronic battles against depression, anxiety, or similar maladies. From your perspective, this chapter might come across as overly simplistic. Believe me, I understand where you're coming from. I struggled with depression and anxiety for many years. My own battle stemmed from my upbringing as well as a genetic predisposition which I inherited from my mom. I have learned the importance of a well-rounded strategy to win this battle, a strategy that might include Christian counseling, lifestyle changes, and medical treatment to remedy physiological factors such as hormonal deficiencies.

While these chapters are not a cure-all for complex emotional struggles like chronic depression, they cover a foundational truth essential to recovery: To win the battle for our emotions, we must win the battle for our minds. That is, we must learn to think right in order to feel right. You'll hear that principle espoused in one form or another by any counselor, Christian and non-Christian alike.

That's why we who follow Christ are so richly blessed. God has given to us the gift of Scripture, a storehouse of rich, hope-filled truth which has the power to transform our thoughts and shape our attitudes. Translating truth to praise is a powerful and practical way to begin reprogramming our minds which, in time, will lead to the emotional healing we long for.

Okay, are you ready to leave the darkness and start living in the light? Then let the training begin.

Chapter 7

Tuning Our Hearts for Praise

As Jesus has shown us, we can choose to see a bunch of dumb birds pecking in the grass, or we can see evidence of our Heavenly Father's intimate involvement in the world, how he moves the levers of creation to feed the tiniest bird. This simple yet profound insight is the inspiration behind the first step in our training: Make up your mind to see the world around you as Jesus sees it.

In fact, let's make this very practical: Go on a praise-walk several times every day and recount all the ways God has shown his goodness. If you're at home, stroll through the rooms and hallways and look for evidence of God's watch-care over you. Then thank the Lord aloud for a warm place to live, for the food which fills your refrigerator and cupboards. When you see the portraits on the wall, recount all the good memories you've enjoyed with your family, and how this, too, is a gift from the Lord.

Personally, I used to go on praise-walks at work when my job permitted me to step outside and walk around the office building. I'd thank God for the beautiful day. I'd thank him that I have a job which enabled me to provide for my family. And on tough days, I'd thank him for using the challenges to mold my character. I'd recall the friendships I enjoyed among my coworkers and how I benefited professionally and personally from their influence.

When I'm at church, I can look around and see abundant reasons for praise as well: The Lord has given us a pastor who preaches the truth of Scripture. I see dozens of volunteers working hard to keep the ministries running. I rejoice in the family-spirit within our congregation. And I express gratitude to God for the brothers and sisters in Christ who have ministered to my family and me in personal ways—and the list goes on.

Time and again, I have seen in my own life how determined, persistent praise can overcome bouts of negative emotions, such as roiling resentment or paralyzing anxiety. Those victories have confirmed my hunch that the Devil is behind many of those attacks. After all, the Devil is a "roaring lion" who prowls around, looking for someone to intimidate (1 Peter 5:8). Just as King David's harp could send demons away, our praise can have the same effect. (See 1 Samuel 16:23.) The Devil, who loathes hearing God glorified, will endure our triumphant song only so long before he decides it's not worth the effort, and he will flee (James 4:7).

Speaking of David and his harp, this brings us to our next training exercise: immersing ourselves in the power of God-honoring music. Not only is music amazingly effective in reshaping our hearts, it can also be great fun. If the word "fun" sounds inappropriate, it's simply shorthand for the joyful pleasure that comes from knowing the Lord on a heart-to-heart level. The Psalms, in fact, often portray worship as a passionate experience where fervent celebration, dancing, and shouting are welcome. (See Psalm 149.) Intrigued? Then let's strike up the band.

Music: Language of the Heart

If you're eager to shine as one of God's stars in the night sky, then underline this next statement: Fill your life with joyful, God-honoring music. This bit of wisdom comes from none other than the apostle Paul. "Be filled with the Holy Spirit, *singing psalms and hymns and spiritual songs among yourselves, and making music to the Lord in your hearts.* And give thanks for everything to God the Father in the name of our Lord Jesus Christ." (Ephesians 5:18-20, NLT) Paul understood that good music honors the Lord and nourishes our souls.

The Lord gave us the gift of music as a vital means to express our hearts to him. That's why he placed a large musical anthology right in the middle of our Bibles—the book of Psalms, containing the lyrics of a hundred and fifty songs. We know these poems were sung to music because we find notations throughout like this one: "For the choir director: A psalm of David, to be sung to the tune 'Doe of the Dawn.'" (Psalm 22, NLT)

The Psalms teach us volumes about musical praise. Their emotional range covers the spectrum from mournful to ecstatic. Some psalms are deeply personal, focused on one struggling believer. Others are global, even cosmic in scale, their sweeping lyrics covering all time and eternity. They are prophetic, poetic, sometimes hard to understand, sometimes repetitive. Some convey truth with childlike vocabulary, others with deep, mysterious imagery. And the last psalm (Psalm 150) lists all sorts of musical instruments which comprised the praise band.

The variety in the Psalms reminds us there is no "one correct style" of Christian music. God is pleased when anyone with a genuine heart expresses his adoration for him, whether through the soaring notes of a pipe organ or the crunchy chords of an electric guitar. It's hard to argue what style of music is most sacred when we have no idea what the praise band sounded like when the Psalms were written. Song lyrics, of course, must be rooted in God's timeless truth expressed in Scripture, but you are free to pick a musical style you enjoy.

Personally, Christian music has had a profound impact on my walk with God. Like a romantic sonnet, a song can soften my heart toward the Lord. Numerous times sacred music has rescued me from the despair this world can bring. If I binge on the news, spend too much time on social media, or soak in the negativity of people around me, my heart begins to shrivel, and the world becomes a dark place. But when I hear a beautiful praise song and it gets into my bloodstream, suddenly the light of Christ brightens my horizons.

I'm grateful to God we live in an age when we can readily experience the blessing of song, even if we lack musical talent. Our local Christian radio station has introduced me to many inspiring songs composed by contemporary Christian artists—modern psalmists if you will—who are wonderfully skilled at stirring our hearts with the rich wonders of our God.

If music is not an important part of your Christian walk, I urge you to try the following experiment. For one week, listen to Christian music for a little while every day. Locate a radio station in your area that plays Christian music. Or stream one over the internet. Or dig out those music albums you haven't listened to in ages. Choose whatever musical style appeals to you. Make sure you *enjoy* listening to the music. Again, don't let anyone tell you one musical style is superior to another. The variety in the Psalms belies the cookie-cutter approach to music.

During this one-week exercise, consider, replacing much of your media consumption (especially news and social media) with Christian music. And let's see how it impacts your relationship with the Lord. Be amazed as your heart becomes a wellspring of gratitude. Let the music chase away those demons you've been battling—

depression, discouragement, loneliness, and anxiety. You'll understand why the Psalmist exclaimed, "It is good to give thanks to the LORD, to sing praises to the Most High. It is good to proclaim your unfailing love in the morning, your faithfulness in the evening..." (Psalm 92:1-2, NLT)

Did you notice, in that last quote, how the psalmist began and ended his day with worship, proclaiming the Lord's love in the morning and his faithfulness at night? That gives us something to think about, doesn't it? How do we begin and end each day? By grabbing our smartphone? (Can't those emails wait?) By updating our Facebook status? (Does the world need to know what you had for breakfast?) By tuning into the morning news shows? (You're not the president. You don't need a national briefing every morning. God has the world under control.)

Here's what's most important as we begin and end each day: We need to open the eyes of our hearts until we see, once again, that our loving, almighty Heavenly Father remains enthroned over the universe. And music is a wonderful gift from heaven to keep our vision clear.

Nothing but Praise

As I have aspired to grow in genuine gratitude toward the Lord, an interesting transformation has happened in my life: In the past, whenever I was beset with negative emotions, I'd grovel before the Lord, asking for deliverance. "O Lord, help me face one more day at the office ... O Lord, help me keep my patience with the kids ... O Lord, please provide for our financial needs...!" Lately, however, I've learned to approach these battles quite differently. Instead of crying out to the Lord like a helpless victim, I'm learning to praise him like a confident warrior. I choose to embrace by faith what God has promised—that in Christ we are victors (Romans 8:37).

In the book of Acts, the young Jerusalem church exemplified these kinds of prayers. As the tide of persecution rose against them, they gathered together and proclaimed to heaven, "Master, You are the One who made the heaven, the earth, and the sea, and everything in them." (Acts 4:24, HCSB) Notice how they began, not with all the horrible things their enemies had done, but with all the amazing things their God had done. They affirmed that he was the God who created all things.

Then they acknowledged God's sovereign control over history: "You [Lord] said through the Holy Spirit, by the mouth of our father David Your servant: 'Why did the Gentiles rage and the peoples plot futile things?'" (Acts 4:25, HCSB) In other words, the persecution against the early church was no surprise to the Lord. In fact, he had revealed to King David, centuries before, that the world would rage against God and his people. (See Psalm 2.) God was firmly in control of world events, and this truth filled the praises of the Jerusalem church.

This kind of praying seemed to be a pattern among the early Christians. When Paul and Silas visited Philippi as missionaries, a mob rose up, beat them, and threw them into prison. While in shackles, we find Paul and Silas "praying and *singing hymns* to God." (Acts 16:25, HCSB) Again, praise saturated their prayers. Paul's example in Philippi only underscores his credibility when he encourages us toward a lifestyle of praise as well.

> *Rejoice* in the Lord always. I will say it again: *Rejoice!* ... Don't worry about anything, but *in everything*, through prayer and petition *with thanksgiving*, let your requests be made known to God. And the peace of God, which surpasses every thought, will guard your hearts and minds in Christ Jesus.

> (Philippians 4:4-7, HCSB)

Did you notice the pattern as well as the blessing? The pattern: Rejoice always. Pray with thanksgiving in everything. Then the blessing: "And the peace of God ... will guard your hearts and minds in Christ Jesus."

Here, then, is the challenge: The next time crushing circumstances drive us to prayer, instead of pleading to God as desperate beggars, let us commit to praising him as confident victors. That's right. Approach him with *nothing but praise.* How long can we go just praising and thanking him? Five minutes? Ten minutes? In time, as our hearts swell with gratitude, we'll find inspiration for praise all around us.

We'll praise him for the treasures we have right now in Christ Jesus.

We'll praise him for answered prayers.

We'll praise him for the unspeakable joy waiting for us in glory.

We'll praise him for the day-to-day faithfulness in our lives.

We'll praise him for all the life-lessons he has taught us during our walk with Christ.

We'll praise him for our wonderful brothers and sisters in Christ who have so blessed us.

We'll speak right back to God, with conviction, the promises he has given us in Scripture, celebrating their certain fulfillment.

We'll praise him. We'll thank him. And we'll praise him again.

When we immerse ourselves in praise, we'll soon find ourselves in the presence of our loving Heavenly Father who has assured us he knows what we need even before we ask him (Matthew 6:8). That's the peace of God which surpasses all understanding. And in that moment, we'll wonder why we were so worried in the first place.

Inhale Scripture, Exhale Praise

For those who are eager to embark on this lifelong journey of praise, I commend to you the best teachers I know—all the men and women whose praises fill the pages of Scripture, both Old and New Testaments. Sit at their feet, absorb their passion, hear their praise, and emulate their examples. In short, inhale Scripture, exhale praise … inhale Scripture, exhale praise. Repeat for a lifetime.

In the New Testament, for example, you'll find rich verses of praise penned by the apostles who, time and again, break into heartfelt thanksgiving over God's lavish generosity through Christ. Consider how Peter opens his first letter:

> All praise to God, the Father of our Lord Jesus Christ. It is by his great mercy that we have been born again, because God raised Jesus Christ from the dead. Now we live with great expectation, and we have a priceless inheritance—an inheritance that is kept in heaven for you, pure and undefiled, beyond the reach of change and decay. And through your faith, God is protecting you by his power until you receive this salvation, which is ready to be revealed on the last day for all to see.
>
> (1 Peter 1:3-5, NLT)

Can you sense the deep currents of joy running through Peter's doxology? (If not, go back and read it again. Aloud! *With feeling this time!*) When you find praise-inspiring passages like this, highlight them, underline them, take notes, and let them saturate your thinking. Better yet, adopt them as your own and speak those verses right back to God in grateful thanksgiving.

Peter has shown us how to fix our hearts on what is eternally true about us in Christ. Through praise, we lay hold of what is unseen, because what is unseen is eternal. What is seen is only temporary. (See 2 Corinthians 4:18.) Then, we will experience a growing measure of heaven's joy because we realize our true identity is not the person we see in the mirror but the person we will become when Christ returns, as Paul explains:

> Since you have been raised to new life with Christ, set your sights on the realities of heaven, where Christ sits in the place of honor at God's right hand. *Think about the things of heaven, not the things of earth. For you died to this life, and your real life is hidden with Christ in God.* And when Christ, who is your life, is revealed to the whole world, you will share in all his glory.
>
> (Colossians 3:1-4, NLT)

There are all kinds of praise-passages in Scripture. Often, praise is simply a marvelous expression of God's greatness. In the book of Revelation, we find the angels of heaven are in awe over God's majestic splendor, and they can't help but sing his praises.

> "Holy, holy, holy is the Lord God, the Almighty—
>   the one who always was, who is, and who is still to come ...
> "You are worthy, O Lord our God,
>   to receive glory and honor and power.
> For you created all things,
>   and they exist because you created what you pleased."
>
> (Revelation 4:8, 11, NLT)

> "Great and marvelous are your works,
>   O Lord God, the Almighty.
> Just and true are your ways,

O King of the nations.
Who will not fear you, Lord,
and glorify your name?
For you alone are holy.
All nations will come and worship before you,
	for your righteous deeds have been revealed."

(Revelation 15:3-4, NLT)

Such passages remind us that we can take any truth we've learned about God and offer it back to him through praise. So, when you're studying the Bible and discover (or rediscover) something wonderful about the Lord, perhaps it's time to stop reading and start praising. Stand up, lift your hands high, look to heaven, and start bragging on your Heavenly Father.

If you accept this challenge, you're in for an exciting journey. The prayers and praises of Scripture will become a part of you. Your heart will develop an instinct to kneel and praise the Lord in good times and bad. Soon your heart will compose psalms born out of your own experiences. And you will join the chorus of all those great men and women through the ages who were passionate about the greatness of God. And you'll discover, as they did, how praise transforms any moment into something glorious.

A Look Back and a Look Ahead

As we bring this section to a close, let's take our bearings with a look back and a look ahead. First, a look back: In the early chapters of *The Glorious Ordinary*, we talked about obedience. We learned that God's will for our lives is always right in front of us: Wherever we are, whatever we're doing, he calls us to live out the love and holiness of Jesus. Even the most mundane chore gleams with Heaven's glory when we "put on the Lord Jesus," to use Paul's words (Romans 13:14). So, we've taken a fresh look at *obedience.*

We also immersed ourselves in the glorious news that our Heavenly Father desires a personal relationship with us, and through Jesus Christ, he accomplished all that is necessary to make that possible. Although we'll struggle and stumble in our walk, our Heavenly Father's love and acceptance remain unchanged. He delights in us, not because he finds us useful, but because we are his precious children. That's *relationship.*

Finally, we talked about gratitude. We've learned how we can channel heaven's glory by offering genuine thanksgiving to our Heavenly Father, regardless of our circumstances. In short, we've taken a fresh look at *praise.*

So, there we have it: We've explored *obedience* to God, our *relationship* with God, and our *praise* to God. It seems to me that those three elements form the heart of the first and greatest commandment, that we love the Lord our God with all our heart, mind, soul, and strength. We love God by *obeying* him, by pursuing a *relationship* with him, and by *praising* him. To be sure, the command requires a lifetime of learning and growing, but its essence is wonderfully simple.

Again, don't over-think it.

Don't make it more complicated than it really is.

So, we've come a long way in embracing the first of the two great commandments. As Jesus tells us, it all comes down to loving God and loving people. Let's now turn to that second commandment: Love your neighbor as yourself.

Part 4
The Greatest of These is Love

Now these three remain: faith, hope, and love.
But the greatest of these is love.

-Paul the Apostle
1 Corinthians 13:13
(HCSB)

Chapter 8
The Golden Rule

The second of the two great commandments is this: "Love your neighbor as yourself." Jesus has given us a command so simple, a child could grasp it. And he keeps the scope manageable. He says, "Love your *neighbor*." He does *not* say, "Love everybody." Neither does he say, "Love the whole world." Neither does he ask you to solve world hunger. His focus is small and personal: Love your *neighbor* as yourself. In other words, love the person right in front of you. I like that. Jesus keeps it simple. He keeps it doable.

So, who is my neighbor? *The Merriam-Webster Dictionary* defines a neighbor as "one living or located near another." Notice, my neighbor is not just the guy who lives next door; he's the person *near* me wherever I happen to be. He's the person sitting by me on the bus. He's the co-worker in the next cubicle. He's the cashier at the grocery store. I find this definition harmonizes well with the parable of the Good Samaritan, a story Jesus told in response to the question "Who is my neighbor?" (See Luke 10:25-37.)

Jesus clarifies the command even further by restating it in a slightly different way, "Therefore, whatever you want others to do for you, do also the same for them—this is the Law and the Prophets." (Matthew 7:12, HCSB) These days we call it the Golden Rule: Treat others the way you want to be treated. And, once again, we discover the pathway to glory is wonderful in its simplicity. Anyone humble enough to embrace this unassuming command is on his way to exalted status in the kingdom of God.

I remember clearly when the Golden Rule made a lasting impact on my life. It happened during my high school years when I was a very sarcastic teenager. While the term "sarcastic teenager" is arguably redundant, I was exceptionally gifted. My cutting wit earned both admiration and dismay from my friends, and it served as the perfect camouflage to hide all my insecurities. With one well-aimed jibe, I could slay anyone. I could reduce an entire classroom to laughter with the perfect one-liner. And to keep my arsenal of gags well-supplied, I purchased books full of insults. (Yeah, it was bordering on full-blown psychosis.)

Unfortunately, my cutting wit had a terrible downside: The laughter always came at someone else's expense. Although my victims laughed right along with the crowd, they died a thousand deaths on the inside. I should know. I experienced the same humiliation whenever I got a dose of my own medicine, which happened a lot. That's just the nature of high school. Like everyone else, I'd hide my agony behind a fake smile and a fake laugh.

During those teen years, something else was happening in my life. Not only was I reading my *Book of Insults*, I was also beginning to read my Bible seriously for the first time. And as I absorbed Jesus' teachings in the gospels, the Golden Rule began to weigh on my conscience. I sensed God was confronting me with a pointed question: *Tim, if you hate being publicly humiliated, why are you so eager to humiliate others?* Wow, bullseye. It was the beginning of a profound transformation. I needed to start treating others the way I wanted to be treated.

Ever since then, God has been leading me to root out that streak of cruel sarcasm and to cultivate instead a spirit that encourages others. Granted, it's been a long journey with many lapses along the way, but progress has been steady. I am now light-years from where I started. Thanks to Jesus' command to love my neighbor as myself, I am more inclined to build others up rather than tear them down.

By the way, did you notice how the Golden Rule prompted me to take a hurt and translate it into love? The pain of public humiliation reminded me never to inflict that kind of suffering on others. What an amazing discovery: *Let your hurts teach you how to love.* The Golden Rule, you see, presents us with a choice. We can allow our personal injuries to fester and poison our hearts, or we can welcome the wisdom we gained through hardship. So, the next time someone wounds you with gossip, let it forever remind you to keep your words kind and edifying. When someone lets you down, resolve to show only faithfulness in your relationships. When you feel the sting of unfair criticism, thank your Heavenly Father for the reminder to be thoughtful and fair with your words.

Again, treat others the way you want to be treated. That command alone can propel you a long way toward Christlike maturity. And because love-of-neighbor is the guiding principle within all God's commands, we can maintain the spirit of the law while seeking to follow the letter of the law, just as Paul reminds us: "If you love your neighbor, you will fulfill the requirements of God's law. For the commandments say, 'You must not commit adultery. You must not murder. You must not steal. You must not covet.' These—and other such commandments—are summed up in this one commandment: 'Love your neighbor as yourself.'" (Romans 13:8-9, NLT)

Guaranteed Pathway to Success

As you become acquainted with God's ways, you will make an amazing discovery: If your highest aspiration is to love—to love the

Lord and to love your neighbor—you are on God's pathway to guaranteed success. You'll never have to worry that, in the end, your life will be deemed a failure. As soon as you commit to pursuing what's important to God, you're golden. Success is yours for the having.

You see, in God's eyes, love and kindness are prized virtues. Don't worry if you weren't born with great talent. God doesn't award talent because, after all, he's the one who gave us our talents (1 Corinthians 4:7). He doesn't award charisma, fame, financial prosperity, or job status. But he is happy to exalt the one who chooses to do all things in love, an aspiration within anyone's reach. I remember the day this dawned on me, and it happened, once again, when I was in high school, in gym class, of all places.

As a teenager, I always dreaded gym. For the athletically challenged, gym class is the worst. It's a Darwinian environment where the fast and the strong eat up the slow and the awkward. One day, as I endured the ignominy of another hour of gym, I looked around the ballfield and noticed other classmates who were miserable as well. Some, in fact, had it a lot harder than I did. Not only were they bad athletes, they also struggled with their studies, or they were socially awkward, or they were unattractive, or they dressed funny. All those shortcomings gave the class bullies plenty of ammunition for their relentless teasing.

Suddenly, I saw an amazing opportunity. I can become famous in God's eyes by loving others! Okay, so I don't excel at sports. Is that such a big deal? The fact remains, I'm free to excel in loving my neighbor, the very thing that brings God pleasure. I'll simply treat others how I want to be treated. I can speak encouragement to the kid who is battered from ridicule. I can be the guy who cheers "Good effort!" when someone blows the big play. I can choose to hang out with the guy everyone else ignores. Wow, suddenly gym class was a mission field. What a turnaround, from athletic failure to glorious kingdom servant. I found myself right in the center of God's will. And in life, that's all that matters.

Let this serve as a reminder for our churches as well. Churches can fall into the trap of valuing talent and giftedness over love, and that can lead to pride among those with high profile talents and an inferiority complex among those with modest talents. Paul speaks to the matter plainly in his letter to the Corinthian church. "If I have the gift of prophecy and understand all mysteries and all knowledge, and if I have all faith so that I can move mountains but do not have love, I am nothing." And he ends with this memorable line, "Now these three remain: faith, hope, and love. But the greatest of these is love." (1 Corinthians 13:2, 13; HCSB)

Be encouraged. Whether we have a spotlight kind of talent or a quiet, behind-the-scenes kind of talent, greatness awaits anyone who aspires to grow in love.

Do All Things with Love

Okay, it's time to sit up straight and pay special attention. I don't want you to miss what's coming because we stand on the verge of launching your ordinary life into the stratosphere of glory. Ready? Here we go.

We have just learned that loving our neighbor is near and dear to God's heart. On God's scale of priorities, loving our neighbor runs a close second to loving God himself. In fact, the two are inseparable as the apostle John reminds us, "For the person who does not love his brother he has seen cannot love the God he has not seen." (1 John 4:20, HCSB) With that in mind, consider this little gem written by Paul: "Do everything with love." This is too important to miss, so here it is again.

*"Do **everything** with love."*
-1 Corinthians 16:14, NLT

In that one verse, God has shown us how to bestow glory on *everything* we do. We simply translate what we're doing right now into an expression of love. Every moment we interact *with* people or do something *for* people, we have an opportunity to love our neighbor. The possibilities are endless, inspiring all sorts of questions: How do I perform my work at the office *with love?* How do I manage a home *with love?* How do I teach a Sunday school class *with love?* How do I shop at Walmart *with love?* How do I discipline our children *with love?* How do I commute to work *with love?*

Not long ago, I arrived early at church one morning to prepare for the Sunday school class I teach. As I passed through the lobby, I found Lloyd, a member of the property committee, standing on a stepladder changing a lightbulb. He greeted me with a smile, and I noticed he was taking real pleasure in his work. He asked me if I had sufficient light in my classroom, and I said yes. He happily informed me they had repainted the room and spoke of additional plans to brighten things up. He exhibited the spirit of a servant: *I want to do whatever I can to help you in your teaching ministry.*

Think of it: Brother Lloyd proved you can change a lightbulb *with love!*

People who bring a spirit of love and humility to their work inspire me, no matter how big or how small the task. "Do everything with love." It's a very simple command yet wonderfully refreshing because it compels us to root out all the lesser motivations that rob our hearts of joy—motivations like guilt, peer pressure, legalism, or empty tradition.

So, how do we go about transforming an ordinary activity into an expression of love? Admittedly, attempting to encapsulate the concept of love in a few paragraphs is akin to writing a history of the world on a napkin, but I have found a handful of truths in Scripture which guide me in transforming an ordinary chore into an expression of love.

First, whatever I'm doing, I must bring to the task the heart of a *servant.* That is, I'm attuned to the need of my neighbor, and I seek to serve that need. I ask myself, how does this task impart goodness to my neighbor? How is it a help to them? What need am I meeting? That's the spirit of servanthood. When I approach any task as an opportunity to help others, the Lord is pleased. Not only that, it fans my enthusiasm for the task at hand.

As I write this paragraph, it's close to Christmas time. My wife Megan, along with her friend Esther, are working hard to organize a nice Christmas banquet for the ladies at our church. I've been encouraged when I hear Megan talk about why the banquet is important. As a young mom, she knows firsthand what a blessing it is to escape the house and kids for a little while and enjoy a special occasion with her sisters in Christ. It's like a cup of cold water to a weary soul. That's what Megan wants to provide for the women, a special evening that lifts their spirits and allows them to deepen their relationships with one another. That's a picture of performing a task "with love," bringing to the work a servant's desire to help or to meet a need in someone's life.

Once we assume the perspective of a servant, the most mundane chore takes on heavenly importance: *I show up early at the office to shovel snow and ice from the sidewalks to provide my fellow workers a safe work environment...At home when dinner is over, I choose to clear the table and load the dishwasher for my wife. She's so busy all day taking care of the kids, I want to help her carry the load...Behind the fast food counter where I work, I always deliver the meals with a smile and a warm 'thank you.' It's my way of bringing a touch of kindness to the lives of our customers...I work the soundboard at church. The Sunday morning service is our best opportunity to encourage the hearts of our church family, so I work hard to make sure the sound system runs smoothly....* Opportunities, you'll discover, are endless.

Now for the second bit of wisdom: Because love, in its most basic form, is treating others how I would want to be treated, **I will put myself in the shoes of my neighbor.** I must learn to see the situation from his perspective, to consider his interests, his thoughts, and his feelings. The word that comes to mind is *empathy*, a virtue closely related to what the New Testament calls *tenderheartedness* (Ephesians 4:32, NASB).

Not long ago, someone rang our doorbell. I opened the front door to find a young man asking if I'd be interested in switching to a more affordable cable-TV package. Now, let's be honest, a salesman at the front door ranks high on the list of life's irritants, right up there with telemarketers who call at dinnertime. So, my first impulse was to be a little bit of a jerk, to dismiss the guy with a snarky reply and close the door before he could launch into his sales pitch.

On that day, however, I chose empathy over rudeness. Once I put myself in the shoes of that salesman, my attitude began to change. No doubt the guy had already endured some rude rejections that afternoon. (In my previous job, I sometimes dealt with angry customers on the phone, so I could relate to his pain.) I realized, as well, the guy is working hard on a hot day to pay the bills. That deserves some respect. And I wondered, is he trying to support a family? Is he having a bad day? Is he stuck in a job he doesn't like? Does he need one more guy piling on and treating him rudely...?

As someone has wisely said, "Be kind, for everyone you meet is fighting a battle you know nothing about."

So, my heart softened toward the salesman, and I chose to respond with a smile and a generous helping of courtesy. I told him thanks for stopping by, but I really wasn't interested in switching cable companies at this time, even to save a few bucks. (It's just such a hassle.) As he left, I wished him a good day. (On those occasions when a salesman is obstinate, I'm learning to maintain a courteous spirit while letting him know our conversation is now over, thank you very much. It's possible to be both considerate and frank.) Again, learning to *empathize* with our neighbor goes a long way in developing a Golden-Rule lifestyle.

Finally, here's a third way to transform a mundane task into something glorious: **Bring to the task a *loving spirit.*** In other words, attitude matters. Suppose my wife is exhausted from taking care of the kids all day. To help her out, I choose to clean the kitchen after supper and bathe the kids. That's a wonderful act of love—unless, of course, I'm griping and complaining about it the whole time. That's the difference between a chore and an act of love. For me, the most helpful description of a loving, Christlike attitude is found in Paul's letter to the Galatian church: "The fruit of the Spirit is love, joy, peace, patience, kindness, goodness, faith, gentleness, self-control." (Galatians 5:22-23, HSCB)

Let's reflect on those winsome virtues for a moment. Imagine what you'll be doing the rest of the day, once you're done reading this fine book. Perhaps you'll cook supper for the family, clean house, mow the lawn, or rush off to a meeting at church. Now, ask yourself: As you go about all those normal activities, how might your attitude and conduct be transformed if you embodied all those Spirit-inspired qualities such as peace, patience, kindness, gentleness, and self-control? Below you'll find a descriptive paraphrase of each quality to guide your thinking.

- Love: Your actions spring from a deep-down devotion to the wellbeing of others.
- Peace: People sense the tranquility and contentment in your heart.
- Patience: You don't let the little stuff get to you. You keep your poise even when circumstances are tough.

- Kindness: You are thoughtful. Being good to others brings you pleasure.
- Gentleness: You are strong, but it's a quiet strength. You have a soft touch, rather than a harsh spirit. Your humility and tender heart come through.
- Self-Control: You are master of your words and actions. You show amazing restraint when others would be flying off the handle.

I must confess, as I reflect on each of those virtues, my emotions are all over the place. I feel convicted, challenged, but also inspired. Something rises inside me and says, "That's the kind of man I want to be." When people see me, watch me, and hear me, I want them to catch a glimpse of God's loving heart.

So, we now have three reminders to guide us in transforming an ordinary task into an expression of love:

1. With a servant's heart, I'll ask how this task meets someone's need, serves someone's best interests, or provides goodness to them.
2. With an empathetic heart, I'll put myself in the shoes of my neighbor and seek to understand what his best interests are, what he's thinking, and how he's feeling.
3. And with a Spirit-filled heart, I'll go about this task with a loving attitude, serving with patience, kindness, joy, and peace.

A Wonderful Life

The second-greatest commandment, much like the first, is wonderfully simple: Treat others the way you want to be treated. And because it's enormously relevant to our most ordinary moments, it opens the way to spectacular glory.

As we travel the glorious road, however, we'll likely discover the journey is far more challenging than we expected. At first glance, the command to love my neighbor seems so basic. It's Dr. Seuss theology. It's like the beginner's slope at the ski resort. But here's the painful truth: Even on this "beginner's slope," we'll wipe out in the trees over and over. And in our most discouraging moments, we'll wonder if the pathway to glory is so accessible after all.

Speaking personally, I confess to having wiped out in the trees quite a few times, but I've found a passage of Scripture that keeps me encouraged. Even though the Lord calls us to set our eyes on perfection (Matthew 5:48), he doesn't *demand* perfection. In fact, he is so kind and merciful, he has promised to reward us for *making progress* toward Christlike maturity as Peter explains:

> Make every effort to respond to God's promises. Supplement your faith with a generous provision of moral excellence, and moral excellence with knowledge, and knowledge with self-control, and self-control with patient endurance, and patient endurance with godliness, and godliness with **brotherly affection**, and brotherly affection with **love for everyone**.
>
> **The more you grow like this,** the more productive and useful you will be in your knowledge of our Lord Jesus Christ ... Then **God will give you a grand entrance** into the eternal Kingdom of our Lord and Savior Jesus Christ.
>
> (2 Peter 1:5-11, NLT)

Did you see the blessing in Peter's words? "A grand entrance" into God's eternal kingdom awaits those who are steadily growing in love. That means each of us has the opportunity to walk through heaven's gates to the sound of applause. The Lord bestows glory on those who are devoted, however imperfectly, to living out the two great commandments: Love God and love your neighbor. No wonder Peter concludes his letter with this strong admonition, "*Grow* in the grace and knowledge of our Lord and Savior Jesus Christ." (2 Peter 3:18, NLT)

If you're like me, you're a long way from earning an A+ when it comes to loving others. (Only Jesus Christ, when he walked among us, earned the A+.) Nevertheless, when God periodically hands me my report card, whatever my grade, I look for this handwritten note: *Great Improvement!* If I'm a better lover-of-people today than I was a year ago, I know the Lord is pleased, and I know I'm on the path that leads to a life well-lived.

Deep down, wouldn't you agree that's what most of us want, to know our lives meant something in the grand scheme of things? That's why Frank Capra's 1946 movie *It's a Wonderful Life,* a perennial Christmas favorite, continues to inspire. It speaks to our soulful longing for a meaningful life. The movie follows George Bailey, a talented and ambitious young man who has a world of opportunity before him. But one twist of fate after another keeps him locked into his small hometown of Bedford Falls, and year after year, he watches all his big chances evaporate. He's destined to remain at home, running his father's failing business, while friends and family head off to pursue their dreams.

Finally, George hits rock bottom. Convinced he's an utter failure, he considers jumping into an icy river to bring his miserable life to an end. If you've seen the movie, however, you know his story does not end there. Little does he know that heaven has been watching his travails all those years. And in that pivotal moment when George wavers between choosing life or death, an angel named Clarence is sent to intervene.

Clarence, who appears as an amiable old man, spares George's life, but then he does something even more amazing: He shows George what the world would have been like had he never been born.

Thoroughly dumbfounded, George stumbles through this alternate reality, a Bedford Falls where George Bailey never existed. He is horrified to discover that his hometown, without his influence, has become a terribly dark place. He finally understands that his life has been a blessing to others, in ways he never imagined. George now sees his life from heaven's perspective, and he longs for a second chance. He begs Clarence to send him back to the Bedford Falls he's always known.

As soon as Clarence grants his wish, George Bailey blissfully runs through the streets of his beloved hometown—his *real* hometown. He beams with elation because he now knows his life is not a failure after all. In the final scene, we find him at home by the Christmas tree, happily surrounded by family and friends. He then finds a note Clarence has left behind, "Dear George, remember, no man is a failure who has friends."

Whatever theological quibbles we might find in the movie, *It's a Wonderful Life* speaks with power to that profound desire in all of us: We long for someone to tell us that our time in this world has meant something, that we have not wasted our lives after all.

If, like George Bailey, you're despairing because your life seems insignificant, you don't need to wait for Clarence the angel. Jesus Christ has already come to your rescue. He has shown you how to live a wonderful life of breathtaking glory, and the doorway stands open for anyone willing to step through. The message Jesus has given is simply this: "No man is a failure who loves."

Love your neighbor as yourself.

Everywhere you go.

And in God's eyes, your life will be a splendid success, a very wonderful life.

Chapter 9

Love Without Borders

As we've seen, the second greatest commandment applies to every facet of our lives. "Do *everything* with love," Paul writes. And Jesus admonishes us, "*In everything*, therefore, treat people the same way you want them to treat you, for this is the Law and the Prophets." (Matthew 7:12, NASB) It's worth highlighting that all-important phrase: *in everything.*

This calls for some honest soul-searching because many of us, without even realizing it, have absorbed the wisdom of the streets and designated parts of our lives as love-free zones. For example, some have designated the marketplace as a love-free zone. ("Hey, it's not personal, it's business.") For others, it's the workplace. ("Get over it. I'm your boss, not your best friend.") For others, it's the ballfield. ("Hey, I'm just the competitive type.") Or it's the home. ("Stop whining. I'm treating you no worse than my dad treated me when I was a kid.") Or it's what we post on social media. ("Hey moron, you're a shill for the [*insert name of political party*]!")

It's common for people to excuse their unloving attitudes with shallow excuses: "Well, that's just who I am." Or, "It's how everyone else behaves around here." Or, "That's just how I was raised." Regardless, we must exchange our earthly rationalizations for Jesus' eternal wisdom: We are to love our neighbor *in all things.* Not *most* things. *In all things.* So, in this chapter, we'll examine some common venues where people exempt themselves from the second greatest commandment.

Be forewarned. Some of us might experience discomfort as we open doors we'd rather keep closed. I urge you, though, to welcome the pain as God's loving discipline. Let his light shine into those dark corners you've kept hidden. As we've said before, he loves you too much to let you settle for the cheap, shallow principles embraced by the world. There's a higher road he calls you to travel, one that leads to eternal acclaim.

The Marketplace

In the marketplace, the Golden Rule gets squeezed out by all sorts of ugly substitutes: "It's not personal, it's business." "Buyer beware." Behind all these maxims is the assumption that the marketplace enjoys a Golden-Rule exemption.

Shortly after I graduated from seminary, a friend of mine named John approached me for advice. He had just put his car on the market and would soon meet with prospective buyers. The car, he admitted, had some maintenance issues that would likely cause problems in the future. So, here was John's question: Should he disclose the problems voluntarily, or was it okay to remain quiet about them unless specifically asked? Now, John wasn't trying to be sneaky. He was a Christian and wanted to do the right thing, which is why he sought my counsel. He was experiencing the internal angst that happens when we realize the moral code we've inherited from the streets stands opposed to the wisdom from heaven.

So how did I answer his question? Honestly, I replied with a tangled mess of theological lawyerese. I still had too much seminary in me to see how simple the answer was. Really, it comes down to this: Treat others the way you want to be treated. So, here's how I *should* have replied: "John, put yourself in the shoes of the man buying your car. Before you lay down the money, would you want the seller to disclose upfront these maintenance issues?"

"Yeah, I would."

"What if he chose not to? Two weeks after you buy the car, you discover all the problems the seller hadn't disclosed. Would you feel cheated?"

"Probably so."

"There's your answer. Jesus calls us to treat others the way we want to be treated. If you'd feel cheated as the buyer, then what you're doing as the seller is wrong by your own standards."

Notice the transformation. As soon as John places himself in the shoes of his neighbor, the moral question becomes clear. Love rises above self. Love is not content to ask, "Is this good for my wallet?" Love wants to know, "Is this good for my neighbor?" It seems to me the whole field of business ethics has gotten way too complicated. The second greatest commandment brings amazing clarity to our moral quandaries.

I realize many who are savvy in the marketplace will balk at this "unrealistic" code of conduct. Yet here's the irony: The businessman who lives by shady practices will scream bloody murder when he gets duped by someone employing the very same philosophy. His protests betray his hypocrisy. And tragically, he has missed the opportunity to invite heaven's glory into how he does business. Furthermore, he has placed himself in grave peril before God. Let me explain.

Scripture teaches that anyone who maximizes profits at the expense of the Golden Rule is flirting with idolatry. I know the word idolatry gets overused in some of our Bible teaching, but God himself is the one who links greed with idolatry. (See Ephesians 5:5.) You see, we have a choice in life, to bow the knee to Almighty God or bow the knee to the almighty dollar. When we worship God, our first consideration in all things is, "What is God's will in this matter?" If we worship the dollar, our first consideration is, "How will this affect me financially?" While the almighty dollar did not appear at Mount Sinai, it comes bearing a tablet of laws nonetheless. That's why Jesus tells us to make a choice: Serve Almighty God or serve the almighty dollar. You can't do both (Matthew 6:24).

By the way, none of this is to imply that it's a sin to be financially prosperous. Many great men of God were wealthy in their day: Abraham, Joseph, and Job come to mind. But they were men of integrity who honored God above all. That should be our focus as well. Our job is to be men and women who walk the glorious pathway of the Golden Rule. Whether we prosper financially or not, we'll leave that to God. In the meantime, we'll keep our eyes fixed on the eternal reward God has stored up for us in glory.

The Workplace

Closely related to the marketplace is the workplace where, once again, all sorts of worldly maxims prevail. "Business is business." "He who has the gold makes the rules." "Grow or die." "Nice guys finish last." "Sales fixes everything." All these bits of worldly wisdom, at their core, have chosen to prioritize something other than the two great commandments— usually, it's maximizing cash flow, growing the business, or beating the competition. When any one of these things becomes priority number-one, we become the foolish man building our lives on a weak foundation, one that will not survive God's scrutiny (Matthew 7:24-27).

Let's imagine a businessman who has chosen to turn his back on all the worldly business philosophies and embraces the second greatest commandment. Consider what that transformation would look like. First, he commits to treating everyone—clients, customers, vendors, and employees—as he would want to be treated. Beginning with sales, he asks himself, "What does it mean for our sales department to live by the Golden Rule? What does it mean for a salesman to treat a customer the way he'd want to be treated? Hmmm."

Soon our businessman begins to view sales in a whole new way. "Whenever I'm the prospective buyer, I value the salesman who's honest with me. I like the guy who's an expert on his product and views himself as a resource to benefit me, the customer. If his product is not a good fit, he'll tell me so. I don't like high pressure. Give me space to make a careful decision. And I hate smarmy sales pitches that reek of flattery. I like a guy who under-promises and over-delivers, not the other way around." And just like that, this businessman's heartfelt desire to obey the Golden Rule has transformed sales into a sacred endeavor.

But he doesn't stop there. The Golden Rule also impacts how he treats his employees. He needs to overcome the temptation to view his workers as mere resources—expendable cogs in a big machine. "Hmmm," he quietly ponders, "if I were an employee in this business, would I want to work for me?" He thinks back to his younger years when he was a "lowly peon" just starting out in the work-world. "What qualities did I value in a boss? How did I want to be treated? Am I the kind of boss I always wanted to work for?"

Many in the work-world will balk at this "unrealistic" business philosophy. But here's where they've gone wrong: Their standards of success are tragically earthbound. They forget that life is prologue to eternity. Yes, the world-savvy businessman might earn a spot on the Forbes list of the top 100 companies, but all those accolades will come to a jarring end the day of his funeral. He'll exit this world knowing his best days are behind him. He'll have eternity to reflect on Jesus' sobering warning, "What does it profit a man to gain the whole world, and forfeit his soul?" (Mark 8:36, NASB)

Not so for the businessman who has embraced God's righteous ways. Even if the Golden Rule places him at a disadvantage with his competitors, he can rejoice in knowing God has declared him a sterling success. Whether the business grows like gangbusters or remains a small operation, what really matters is that it became a sacred enterprise in God's eyes, and that's all that matters. And this businessman, as he nears the end of his life, knows his best days are ahead of him. His reward will stretch forever into eternity. Think of it: His short-term business philosophy has yielded an eternal payout. That's good business.

The Athletic Field

When it comes to athletic competition, we must remain committed to the Golden Rule each time we take the field. God does not grant exemptions to those who are exceptionally talented or score the winning goal. We must not paper over unkind or disrespectful behavior in the name of just being competitive. Nowhere has God said, "Winning covers over a multitude of sins." An athlete who taunts and demeans others might win the trophy, but he has lost God's approval. (Oh, and that goes for his parents screaming on the sidelines. He who has ears to hear, let him hear.)

On a personal note, I'm watching fewer professional sports games these days. It seems there's been a population explosion of players with massive egos. (Or maybe I'm just noticing it more.) The showboating, the taunting, the drive to be the center of attention, even the desire to injure opposing players—I've had just about enough.

In contrast, I have great respect for those athletes who approach the game honorably, whether they win or lose: They play hard, they do their job, they help the team—and they do so with good manners. They know that "Do unto others" always applies. Oh, and I admire those good-mannered parents cheering on the sidelines, the ones who understand that raising a kid who loves his neighbor is far, far more important than raising a superstar.

So, to our athletes out there, especially the young ones who aspire to do great things, play hard and play fair. Enjoy using the talents God has given you. Above all, show the world what it looks like when a godly man or woman lives out the Golden Rule on the ballfield. Super Bowl rings, Heisman Trophies, and Olympic Gold Medals will all melt in the coming conflagration, but those who earn God's crown of righteousness will wear it for all eternity. (See 2 Peter 3:7; 1 Corinthians 9:25.)

Our Virtual Community

We also need to evaluate how we're treating our neighbor online. People who never behave rudely when speaking face to face will insult their virtual neighbor when posting a comment on social media. Insults, gossip, and angry rants are all forms of hateful conduct, whether they are typed or spoken. A political disagreement or a doctrinal debate does not grant us immunity to be rude. It's tragic but true: In defending the cause of righteousness, misguided Christians will post comments online which, to be frank, are nothing more than hatred for their neighbor in the name of Jesus.

So, before we post anything on social media, let us put ourselves in the shoes of our virtual neighbor. Imagine saying in person what you are about to post online. And when it comes to spreading embarrassing information, we must ask ourselves, "How would I feel if I was the one in the photo?" Or, "How would I feel if I was the subject of that rumor?"

And don't forget, celebrities are people, too, made in God's image. To spread rumors about them or to post embarrassing pictures of them is wrong, just as it's wrong to do it to a good friend. Some, like the Paparazzi, will argue that celebrities are in the public domain.

Sorry. There are no boundaries to the Golden Rule. Treat everyone as you want to be treated, even if they're famous.

Our Homes

As hard as it is to admit, some of us have designated our homes as love-free zones, the very place where God calls us to show our highest affection and loyalty. For good or for ill, our upbringing has shaped our definition of what's normal behavior in family life, and our reflex is to treat our children, for instance, as we were treated as a kid—the inverse of the Golden Rule. If dad ruled the family with an iron fist, his child will likely do the same once he has a family of his own. The abandoned son becomes the absentee father. The berated daughter becomes the demanding mother. The man raised on scorn will tear down his family with ridicule.

Parents should pause and ask themselves, "Am I treating my kids how I wanted to be treated when I was growing up? Or, out of long-buried resentment, have I resorted to the hurtful behavior I saw in my parents?" I recently found a meme online that expresses the sentiment perfectly: "Be the person you needed growing up."

And when it comes to our families, we must be mindful of the adage, "Familiarity breeds contempt." It's so easy to let those closest to us catch the brunt of our anger. When we leave the house, we put on our best self. But once we come home, the mask comes off and the fangs come out. In those moments, let's pause, take a deep breath, and ask ourselves, "How do I want to be treated in my own home, even when I'm the most unlovable?" Our answers to that question will serve as an excellent code of conduct toward our family, those that God has entrusted to our care.

At Church

It's tragic but true; we can establish love-free zones within our own church. Take the congregational business meeting as an example. A lot of Christians, I've noticed, have two distinct voices: their Sunday morning voice and their business-meeting voice. Their Sunday morning voice is polite, cheerful, and kind. The voice they bring to the business meeting, however, is gruff, demanding—even rude.

Honestly, I have scoured the Bible from cover to cover, and nowhere can I find the church-business-meeting exemption for the Golden Rule. So, at the next congregational business meeting, will you set the example? Will you be the adult in the room whose conduct reminds everyone that love has no boundaries? Remember, a dull, ordinary business meeting becomes glorious in God's eyes when each member speaks to his neighbor with the kind of courtesy he desires for himself.

Another common misstep among Christians is to go to war with each other over theological differences, wielding with abandon the accusation "Heretic!" or "False Teacher!" Again, doctrinal differences do not exempt us from God's command to love. If my brother in the Lord is wrong on a point of doctrine, I will speak to him with the kind of courtesy and charity I desire for myself. Indeed, the Lord wants us to teach one another, correct one another, and help one another to grow toward Christlike maturity. But we are to *speak the truth in love* (Ephesians 4:15). We are to come alongside our brother as a gentle servant, not a quarrelsome judge. (See 2 Timothy 2:23-24.)

While there are essential doctrines we must protect and defend, sometimes at great cost, there are many secondary doctrines where good men will disagree. Even the apostle Peter, in reference to Paul's writings, had to admit, "There are some matters that are hard to understand." (2 Peter 3:16, HCSB) If Peter (the chief apostle!) scratched his head over Scripture, shouldn't we show patience toward a brother who is confused over a point of doctrine? All of us are a work in progress, let's remember, and we should give our brothers and sisters room to figure things out just as God has done for us. I love Paul's attitude toward the Philippians, "Let all who are spiritually mature agree on these things. If you disagree on some point, I believe God will make it plain to you." (Philippians 3:15, NLT)

A Never-Ending Story

All the examples in this chapter bring us back to a seminal truth we've seen before: God never intended for us to label some parts of our lives as spiritual and other parts as secular. All of life is a sanctuary as we learned from Paul in Romans 12:1. No activity is off limits. Likewise, nowhere has God posted a sign that reads "This is a Love-Free Zone."

Without a doubt, the Golden Rule poses a huge challenge, requiring us to swim against the tide at work, in the marketplace, on the ballfield, even at church. On the other hand, the Golden Rule reinforces the liberating message our soul longs to hear: Anyone who truly desires it can live a glorious life. It simply requires loving your neighbor as yourself. Love the person right in front of you, wherever you are.

In everything, love your neighbor as yourself.

In everything.

In everything.

In everything.

Chapter 10
Precious in His Sight

When you placed your faith in Jesus Christ, you joined God's eternal family. The author of Hebrews captures the truth in a single verse: "Jesus and the ones he makes holy have the same Father. That is why Jesus is not ashamed to call them his brothers and sisters." (Hebrews 2:11, NLT) God is now your Heavenly Father. Jesus Christ is your older brother. And we who follow Christ have countless blood-brothers and blood-sisters all over the world.

There's something else you need to know about your eternal family: They are more precious to your Heavenly Father than you can begin to imagine. They are his children after all. He paid an unfathomable price to win them. Because God has such a tender heart toward his family, he takes special notice when you show even the smallest kindness to one of his own. In fact, he views it as a service rendered to him personally. Please don't miss it: *When you serve a fellow Christian in the spirit of love, you are ministering to God personally.*

The writer of Hebrews understood this. "For God is not unjust," he wrote. "He will not forget how hard you have worked for him and how you have shown your love to him by caring for other believers, as you still do." (Hebrews 6:10, NLT) Read and reread that verse until you see it: To help and to serve a fellow Christian is akin to loving God himself. Again,

For God is not unjust.
He will not forget how hard you have worked for him
and how you have shown your love to him
by caring for other believers, as you still do.

-Hebrews 6:10, NLT

All this sheds light on one of Jesus' most dramatic parables, the Parable of the Sheep and the Goats (Matthew 25:31-46). The scene Jesus describes is breathtaking. It's the end of the age. Jesus has returned to earth and sits enthroned as King of the Universe in the company of all the angels and all the nations. Anyone ever born is in attendance, and they watch with expectation as he separates humanity into two groups. Those who are destined to eternal life, he gathers to his right. Those destined for eternal punishment, he gathers to his left.

Jesus then speaks to the sheep on his right. "Come, you who are blessed by My Father, inherit the kingdom prepared for you from the foundation of the world." (v.34, HCSB) Imagine standing there, awash in the Lord's glory, and finally hearing that beautiful invitation. All our bad days are behind us. Only good days lie in front of us as far as the eye can see. Then Jesus goes on to say something astonishing: "For I was hungry and you gave Me something to eat; I was thirsty and you gave Me something to drink; I was a stranger and you took Me in; I was naked and you clothed Me; I was sick and you took care of Me; I was in prison and you visited Me." (vv.35-36)

The Lord's sheep are shocked to hear this. Most of them were not even alive when Jesus walked the earth, so how could he have received their acts of kindness? Confused, they humbly ask him, "Lord, whcn did we see You hungry and feed You, or thirsty and give You something to drink?" (v.37) And here's how Jesus answers: "'I assure you: Whatever you did for one of the least of these brothers of Mine, you did for Me." (v.40) So, who exactly are the "brothers of mine" Jesus refers to? Scripture is clear: He is speaking of our Christian family.

Here's the point, and it's inspiring: When we express love to a fellow brother or sister in Christ, Jesus accepts it as a kindness rendered to him personally. That's the nature of family love. When someone comes to the aid of one member of the family, all the other members are deeply grateful. You do Jesus a personal favor when you help one of his own.

This talk of family brings back a vivid memory. When I was a young teenager, our family traveled to a state park for some horseback riding with friends. My sister Cindy was just a few years old at the time and not ready to handle a horse on her own, so she rode with my mom, happily perched on the front of the saddle. The group had hardly gotten underway when my mom's horse got spooked and started bucking, trying to throw her off. I watched with horror as my mom clung to the saddle for dear life, one hand clutching the saddle horn, the other clutching my sister.

One of our friends, a seasoned horseman, came to the rescue. He walked up and plucked my sister off the saddle like it was no big deal, and then he calmly stepped a safe distance away, my sister wrapped in his arms. Soon the horse settled down, and my mom had kept her saddle the whole time. I still remember welling with gratitude for the guy who rescued my sister. I wanted to hug him, gush all over him, and say thank you. As far as I was concerned, the man who showed courageous kindness toward my sister had ministered to me personally.

Likewise, the heart of Jesus stirs with gratitude whenever someone shows kindness to a member of his family, even if that person is one of "the least of these," that is, someone the rest of the world hardly notices. And what's amazing, as well, is how Jesus recognizes even the smallest act of kindness: "You gave me something to eat ... you gave me something to drink ... you invited me into your home ... you gave me some clothes ... you visited me ... you looked after me..."

As I expressed at the outset of this book, I have a special place in my heart for Christians who fear they'll never measure up in God's eyes unless they accomplish something big and impressive for the kingdom. We are learning, however, that God measures bigness a lot differently than we do. To our Heavenly Father, a small act of kindness toward one of his children is a very big deal. In fact, even a cup of cold water, given to refresh a follower of Jesus, gets heaven's attention. (See Matthew 10:42.) God's kindness and generosity are amazing.

It saddens me, however, when I see Christians working and serving without recognizing the glory right in front of them. Their job at church, as far as they're concerned, is simply one more obligation required to keep the joint running: staff the nursery, keep the building in repair, balance the books, lead the worship service, teach the Sunday school class, and clean the toilets. But these hard-working servants could ignite a fresh fire in their hearts if they simply embraced their ministry as a service to God's beloved people. If God never forgets a cup of cold water given to one of his own, then no ministry is a small thing.

Recently my home church held a special Sunday morning service where ten people were baptized. The pastor asked each one to tell a little of their story before taking the plunge. As I listened to their testimonies, I realized how many invisible ministries are taking place within our church family—invisible to the congregation but not invisible to God. One young mom named Leanne expressed her gratitude to Jim and Nancy, a dear Christian couple who had invited her into their home for fellowship and encouragement many times. A guy named Jon told us how much he valued meeting regularly with Zac and Pastor Bob for Bible study and how that fellowship had strengthened his walk in the Lord. Others were grateful for the friendly, inviting spirit of our church family.

As I listened to their stories, I realized these are the kinds of discreet ministries that God cherishes among his people. I imagined how Jesus might commend each act of kindness: "I was discouraged and lonely, and you invited me into your home. I was limping along in my faith, and you came alongside to strengthen me. I was lost and intimidated coming to a new church, but you made me feel welcome."

And many of those invisible servants will reply, "Lord, when did we see you discouraged or struggling in your faith or lost at church?"

And he'll reply, "Whatever you did for the least of these brothers and sisters of mine, you did it for me. Come and enjoy your reward."

Are you longing to hear that commendation one day? Then I invite you to absorb the stories you are about to read, stories of humble servants who learned to translate their service at church into expressions of love for God's family. The names are fictional, but the truth is real. Each story represents the composite examples of kindhearted servants I've gotten to know over the years. I pray you'll catch their vision.

Cindy the Nursery Worker

Christians tend to view the church nursery as that necessary but inconvenient department where everyone is expected to put in their time. Each week, a few are relegated to babysitting while everyone else gets to do church. Ugh, no wonder nurseries are so hard to staff.

What if we adopted, instead, the attitude of a loving servant I'll call Cindy? Cindy, who raised a houseful of rambunctious kids years ago, is familiar with the grueling challenges of motherhood. That's why she has a special place in her heart for the young moms in her church family. For Cindy, the nursery has become a mission field. When those tired moms show up on Sunday mornings, she greets each one with a smile. She has become the tenderhearted servant she badly needed when she was struggling years ago as a young parent.

She never says the words aloud, but everything about Cindy conveys the gentle message, *I am here to help you. I know you've borne impossible demands throughout the week. You feel like you're about to lose your mind. I've been there, and I feel your pain. Please, let me hold and love your child for a little while so you can focus on the Lord without distraction. And don't hurry back. If you need to linger after the worship service and talk (finally have some adult conversation!) you go right ahead. I'll be here with your precious little one when you get back.*

The Lord has given Cindy the opportunity to live out this beautiful truth: "Carry one another's burdens; in this way you will fulfill the law of Christ." (Galatians 6:2, HCSB) All of us endure seasons of life when our burdens are too much to handle alone, when we need someone to come alongside and say, "Let me help you carry that for a while." For Cindy, that's what nursery is all about.

Mike the Worship Leader

Mike has been leading the church worship band for a few years now. Because the size of their congregation is on the small side of average, finding band members is a challenge. He has done it all: lead vocalist, guitarist, drummer—even keyboardist when they're desperate.

Serving as a worship leader has forced him to do a lot of soul-searching. *What is my job anyway?* At times he has slipped into the mindset of an entertainer, wanting to wow the crowd. Other times he suffocates under feelings of guilt: *Am I doing this out of pride? Are we really giving this our all? Do I even come close to measuring up to the lyrics we're singing? And what's the right music style? If I get too contemporary, the older members complain. If I get too traditional, the younger people complain. There's no winning!*

One day, a passage from the Bible caught Mike's attention, and it caused him to see his role in a whole new way. "For I have great joy and encouragement from your love," Paul wrote to his friend Philemon, "because the hearts of the saints have been refreshed through you, brother." (Philemon v.7, HCSB) Mike sensed the Lord was speaking to him personally: *Be Philemon to your church family. In love, refresh the hearts of God's people.*

That one verse unlocked a stream of new insights about his role as worship leader: *Of course! I will lead worship in a spirit of love for my brothers and sisters in Christ. I will aim to refresh their hearts in the Lord. Through music, I can offer a cup of cold water to a thirsty soul. I can lead them to a place where their hearts find healing. To the weak and weary, I'll be the guy who carries them into the presence of the Lord.*

This has helped Mike escape the entertainment mentality. Instead, leading worship has become an act of compassion. Some in the congregation show up to church beaten down from a grueling week, but when the music opens their hearts to the greatness of God, all those burdens diminish in size. Entering into worship is like stepping under a cool waterfall, where the truth and the Spirit wash all over their parched souls.

Lately, a few teenagers in the congregation have complained about the old hymns in the music lineup. Mike sees this as a symptom of selfishness. These teens need to think beyond their own needs and consider the needs of others. As worship leader, Mike knows his example must embody the spirit of love: He never speaks disparagingly of different music styles; instead, he uses whatever style is required to build up his church family. The hymns speak to the older generation. The contemporary songs speak to the younger. He sings both with enthusiasm, so all are edified. He is willing to be flexible for the sake of meeting the needs of others.

Some in the congregation have criticized him for his approach, saying he is too people-centered, that worship should be God-centered. His response? *Of course our worship is centered on God. We desire to bring honor to his great name. But worship works in two directions. It brings glory to God in heaven, and it builds up his people on earth. Even the apostle Paul instructed his congregations to design their church services with the aim of building up God's people. "All things must be done for edification." (1 Corinthians 14:26, HCSB)*

When you think about it, the role of the worship leader embodies the two great commandments: Love God. And love people. As Mike leads worship Sunday after Sunday, he fully embraces both. God is magnified. And his people are refreshed in the Lord.

Margaret the Financial Supporter

In ten minutes Margaret will leave for Sunday worship, but first she sits down at her kitchen table to write a check for the church. It represents her monthly tithe, the first tenth of her income, which she will place in the offering plate.

As she adds her signature, she recalls how her attitude toward giving has changed over the years. For a long time, it was merely a dry obligation, her church membership dues if you will. Sometimes she was "guilted" into giving during the annual pledge drive. Sometimes it was out of exasperation to help the church meet a financial crisis.

Her heart has changed since then—changed for the better. She'll put that check in the offering plate in a spirit of love. First, it's love for her pastor. God has given the congregation the responsibility to support the pastor and his family. "The laborer is worthy of his wages," said Jesus, speaking of the need to pay ministry workers

(Luke 10:7, NASB). And Margaret wants to do her part. She wants nothing to do with those Christians who force their pastor to live on crumbs even though they are more than able to pay an adequate salary. Jesus has promised that anyone who loves and supports one of his messengers will share in the messenger's reward (Matthew 10:40-42).

In every age, the work of missionaries and pastors have required the financial donations of fellow Christians. Even Jesus required financial support (Luke 8:1-3). The apostle Paul understood this and thanked the Philippian church for their generosity to his ministry: "You have been my partners in spreading the Good News about Christ from the time you first heard it until now." (Philippians 1:5, NLT)

For Margaret, that's exciting. Her donation makes her a partner in all the church's accomplishments for the kingdom. She doesn't have the gift of teaching. The Lord knows she can't sing. But she can give. She makes it possible for others to use their ministry gifts. And she's helping to buy books, maintenance supplies, electricity and gas—not very exciting stuff on the surface, but all essential to the mission. What an opportunity!

So, she writes her check with a heartful of love, choosing to go above and beyond her tithe to give a little extra. As she seals up the offering envelope, she sends up a prayer. *O Lord, thank you that I can give and love in this way. Take my modest offering and use it bless your people and to bring more children into your family through the Gospel message. May those who live in darkness receive the marvelous light of Jesus. Amen.*

Liz the Cleaner of Toilets

Even those who clean the toilets can be famous in God's eyes when they serve in a spirit of love. Just ask Liz, the church janitor. It's her job to keep the church facility sparkling clean, including the restrooms. Each week when she dons her apron, grabs the scrub brush, and leans over the porcelain bowl, she is pleased to follow the example of Jesus. After all, Jesus donned a towel and grabbed a wash basin to clean the dirty feet of his disciples. If Jesus, the King of Glory, demeaned himself for the good of his brothers, who among us is above cleaning toilets?

And if you have any doubt that clean toilets are vital to church life, talk to Liz. She'll ask you a question in return: "Think about the first time you visited our church. Would you have stayed around if the restrooms were on par with those of a cheap gas station?"

You see, Liz knows she's not just cleaning toilets. She's serving her church family. She's providing a clean, inviting place for her brothers and sisters in Christ to gather for fellowship. And she knows, as well, her work is essential to their evangelism ministry; she's removing any possible stumbling block for those who enter the church doors looking for God.

Yes, every child of God has a role in the body of Christ. And no role is a small one when done in the spirit of love.

"Thank You for Your Service!"

If you have found this chapter inspiring, I hope you will share what you've learned with your fellow brothers and sisters in Christ. There are many hardworking Christians who need someone to come alongside and hear the good news that God cherishes their service. Kind words of appreciation are wonderfully encouraging and desperately needed.

So please, as you learn to see your own work through Jesus' eyes, help others do the same. Help them see the goodness they're bestowing on others and how much it means to our Heavenly Father. When you pick your child up from the church nursery, let those dear servants know how much their ministry blesses you. Sunday morning after the service is over, walk up and thank the worship band for their hard work. And when the Lord touches your heart through their music, be sure to tell them, so they can share your joy.

Thank the youth pastor for creating a safe fellowship where your kids can make friends and grow in Christ. Let him know, as a parent, the difference his ministry has made in the life of your child. When you know someone has been praying for you, tell them the good news when God answers. Thank the members of the property committee for providing such an attractive and inviting place for God's family to gather. Thank the bookkeeper for all those unseen hours he spends tracking the church finances.

Recently, the Lord reminded me just how hungry people are for encouragement in their work. Our son Levi attends a Christian preschool, and one day my wife and I received an email from the director who wanted to pass along a funny story:

> Several of the children in class enjoy playing a game in the dramatic play area. They take turns being a bunny, hiding four plastic eggs, and then the others have to find them. It was Levi's turn to be the bunny. A friend said to him, "It's your turn to hop and hide the eggs." Levi replied happily, "I am hopping with the knowledge of my Lord and Savior Jesus Christ!!!!" Your son just makes my heart sing with joy!

As you might expect, Megan and I got a good laugh out of that email. When I sent back my response, I made sure Levi's Sunday school teacher Denise received a copy of the reply. "Thanks for the encouraging email," I wrote. "Yes, Levi keeps us laughing and shaking our heads much of the time. But I have to give credit where credit is due. I think he picked up his Biblical proclamations in his Sunday school class at our church."

A few days later, when I delivered Levi to his Sunday school class, I asked Denise if she had received the email. She had, and she confirmed that, yes, Levi had learned his Biblical proclamations in her class. She thanked me for copying her on the email, saying it had been a huge encouragement. She admitted there are days she wonders how much impact she's having on the kids. She summed up her appreciation for my email with two words, "I cried."

Wow, her reaction surprised me. But, then again, why should it? So many servants of the Lord are out there putting in long hours, doing their best, and struggling against obstacles. And when they become weary, they wonder if their efforts matter. And all it takes is one kindhearted servant to show them how their labor is genuinely helpful to God's family. And suddenly, they're able to see the glory in their service all over again.

Be generous with your encouragement.

Help others see the glory in their service.

Remind them: They're serving the Lord Jesus personally.

Chapter 11

Love Rooted in Wisdom

All around you, glorious opportunities await. No matter where you go, there you find people, and God has called us to love them. When you aspire to love your neighbor as yourself, you are on the road to eternal success. But don't be surprised if you experience disappointment and hard lessons along the way. Let's face it; people are messy. Knowing how to express God's love in this imperfect world requires great wisdom at times. The apostle Paul understood this. "I pray that your love will keep on growing *in knowledge and every kind of discernment,*" he writes, "so that you can approve the things that are superior and can be pure and blameless in the day of Christ." (Philippians 1:9-10, HCSB)

Consider some of the sticky situations Paul had to address as an apostle. On the one hand, he calls us to be kind and generous to those in need (Ephesians 4:28). On the other hand, he warns us not to subsidize laziness (2 Thessalonians 3:10). In other words, love does not enable bad behavior. Love might offer a word of encouragement (1 Thessalonians 5:11). At other times love requires a firm rebuke (Titus 1:13). Love might call for forgiveness and restoration (2

Corinthians 2:7.) Or it might call for confrontation and discipline, "tough love" if you will (1 Corinthians 5:1-4).

Godly love, we must understand, is more than warm fuzzy feelings and being nice to everyone we meet. The principle "Do unto others as you would have them do unto you" serves as an excellent foundation for living out God's love in the world, but building on that foundation is a lifelong process which requires insight and maturity. In this chapter, I draw attention to a handful of truths that will help keep our love rooted in God's wisdom.

True Love Always Conforms to God's Word

This first building block is vital and serves a cornerstone to all the others: *True love always conforms to God's word.* As the apostle John writes, "We know we love God's children if we love God and obey his commandments." (1 John 5:2, NLT) Study John's words closely until you see it: A love which departs from God's commands is not love at all. That's why we can only mature in Christlike love if we become lovers of Scripture, for there God has provided a rich storehouse of truth and wisdom.

Always remember, the command which precedes all others is this: Love the Lord your God with all your heart, with all your soul, with all your mind, and with all your strength. Your love for people must flow out of your love for God. If we truly love God and truly love our neighbor, we will never break God's commands, nor will we encourage our neighbor to do so. "If you love Me, you will keep My commands," says Jesus (John 14:15, HCSB).

Sadly, confusion abounds in this regard. The world at large tries to define love apart from God, and that always leads to disaster. The most obvious distortion is evident all around us, the attempt to define sexual immorality as a kind of love. Unfortunately, many professing Christians have bought the poison. But here is where a clear understanding of God's word rescues us from the deception:

While God created man, woman, and the sexual relationship, including all the romance, passion and pleasure that go with it, he also set clear boundaries for our good. God invites us to enjoy his gift of sex but only within the boundaries of heterosexual marriage. Sex outside those boundaries (such as premarital sex, extramarital sex, or homosexuality) is *not* an expression of true love. It is a man-made counterfeit that leads to regret.

Remember, when God speaks truth to us, he has our best interests at heart. Be a lifelong student of Scripture. Let your love grow deep roots into the rich soil of his word. In the end, you'll be glad you did, and you'll understand the words of the psalmist who wrote many centuries ago, "How I love Your instruction! It is my meditation all day long." (Psalm 119:97, HCSB)

You're Not the Answer to Everyone's Problems

If God has given you a tender heart which is naturally sensitive to the needs of others, this next word of advice is vital: *God does not expect you to meet the need of everyone on the planet.* God knows there are more problems in the world (even in your own neighborhood!) than one person can handle. The impulse to rescue anyone and everyone might feel like the loving thing to do, but it poses a real danger. Our good intentions, when unchecked by God's wisdom, will lead to burnout and disillusionment. So, remain alert to the danger-signs. If resentment and exhaustion begin to characterize your service, you might be taking on more than God intended.

Remember, even Jesus, when serving within the limitations of a human body, was incapable of meeting every need that came along. That required him to draw boundaries, set priorities, and to say no to legitimate needs. Notice, from the Gospel of Mark:

> Very early in the morning, while it was still dark, [Jesus] got up, went out, and made His way to a deserted place. And He

was praying there. Simon and his companions went searching for Him. They found Him and said, "Everyone's looking for You!"

It was barely sunup and crowds were already gathering, all desperate for Jesus' healing touch. The disciples grew alarmed when they saw people multiplying who were crippled, deformed, sick, and demon-possessed. "Lord, everyone is looking for you!" Jesus' response, however, is a bit shocking.

> And He said to them, "Let's go on to the neighboring villages so that I may preach there too. This is why I have come."

(Mark 1:35-38, HCSB)

When Jesus departed Capernaum that day, he left behind many unmet needs. Although he was wonderfully compassionate and ached for hurting crowds, he had to choose his priorities carefully; otherwise, he'd neglect the mission his Heavenly Father had given him, to preach the good news of the kingdom. Jesus said no to the good in order to say yes to his Father's best. We, his followers, will have to do the same.

It's hard to admit it, but no matter how much we give, serve, and sacrifice, there will always be needs left over. And there's an unfortunate tendency among some Christians to blame the church for all the unmet needs in the world. Frankly, that kind of message can demoralize those who are already giving and serving to the best of their ability.

If God the Father did not expect his own son to meet every need that crossed his path, surely God does not expect it from you. Be wise. Resist the temptation to serve out of guilt or pressure. I like Paul's advice on the topic, written to the Corinthian church regarding their contributions to help the poor: "You must each decide in your heart how much to give. And don't give reluctantly or in response to pressure. 'For God loves a person who gives cheerfully.'" (2 Corinthians 9:7, NLT)

By all means, grow in love and generosity, but when your service becomes a burden, step back and re-evaluate. Consider the possibility you've taken on too much. If Jesus in his humanity had to say no to genuine needs, how much more will we? Until Jesus returns and cleans up this huge mess on earth, those are the tough decisions we'll have to make.

Tough Love

The term "tough love," as far as I know, was coined in the twentieth century. The concept, however, is rooted in God's timeless wisdom. Love, at times, will need to be tough, and on those occasions we'll discover that "the loving thing to do" doesn't feel so loving. That's why our love must be built on the foundation of God's word, not in sentimentalism. Consider some of the examples of tough love we find in Scripture:

- Sometimes love requires a rebuke (Luke 17:3).
- Sometimes love requires discipline, as in a parent toward his child (Proverbs 13:24) or an adult toward a fellow brother in the Lord (Matthew 18:15-17).
- Sometimes the loving thing to do is to let someone experience the consequences of his sin (2 Thessalonians 3:10).
- Sometimes love requires separating ourselves from others, for the good of the sinner as well as the good of the community (2 Thessalonians 3:6, 1 Corinthians 5:1-12).
- Love does not settle for shallow, manipulative shows of repentance (Joel 2:12-13). True repentance requires brokenness over one's sin (Psalm 51:17).

When it comes to tough love, always remember that redemption is the goal. We desire and pray that the brother who has strayed from God will learn the right lessons, will experience genuine contrition, and will return to the path of obedience.

That said, when a wandering brother experiences true brokenness over his sin, we welcome him back with open arms and extend forgiveness. We become the tenderhearted father who rejoices at the return of his prodigal son (Luke 15:20). Thus, as we grow in love, we learn how to be tough and tender at the same time, and when you think about it, that's a good description of God's character. True love requires a thick skin and a tender heart.

Be Careful Out There

To hear some people talk, true love is always marked by an aura of warm fuzzy feelings. There's a danger in that kind of thinking. When we define love only in emotional terms, we become vulnerable to deception and the cruelties of the world. You've probably seen it as I have: A well-meaning Christian, who is far too trusting, gets pulled into a toxic relationship with someone who traffics in lies and manipulation. We find this perverse dynamic in all kinds of situations: in new romances, marriages, and friendships, even in churches where the pastor is exploiting the parishioners or (yes, I've seen it) the parishioners are exploiting the pastor.

The human heart is capable of terrible corruption, and it's not unchristian to admit it. It's only prudent. Jesus, the most loving man who ever lived, was a frank realist about human nature. When he commissioned his disciples to preach the Good News all over Galilee, he minced no words: "Look, I'm sending you out like sheep among wolves. Therefore be as shrewd as serpents and as harmless as doves." (Matthew 10:16, HCSB)

Likewise, within that same message, he says, "If anyone will not welcome you or listen to your words, shake the dust off your feet when you leave that house or town." (10:14) According to Jesus, there are times when Gospel messengers will need to say "Goodbye and good riddance."

Even more jarring is this excerpt from Jesus' Sermon on the Mount: "Don't give what is holy to dogs or toss your pearls before pigs, or they will trample them with their feet, turn, and tear you to pieces." (Matthew 7:6, HCSB) The point is, some people are so vile and abusive, it's unwise to offer them the precious, holy truths of God. These pigs, as it were, have no appetite for truth; they only want to devour the giver for their own ends. Jesus, it seems, wants to protect us from unnecessary abuse.

Granted, these hard sayings raise tough questions. When and in what circumstances do we say goodbye and good riddance? And how can we identify the irredeemable pigs of the world without becoming cynics? Answering those questions is not easy. It will require seasoned maturity and sensitivity to the Holy Spirit. Despite the challenges, however, we must take Jesus' warnings seriously. The world is filled with corrupt, abusive people, so our love for others must be guided by discernment and prudence.

I remember, as an adolescent, attending a Sunday school class filled with teenagers. We were discussing Jesus' command to love others, and someone raised this tricky question: Does Jesus want us to pick up hitchhikers along the highway? Admittedly, I was stumped. My parents, I was convinced, would answer "No!" But what would Jesus say?

Having gained a lot of wisdom since then, I know how I'd respond if the topic came up today. I'd urge any group of teenagers— especially the young ladies—not to pick up strangers along the highway. The risk of assault or abduction is too great. "I commend your compassion," I'd say to them. "And I encourage you to keep your eyes open for opportunities to show the love of Christ. People who need his love are all around you. But leave the hitchhikers to those who are better equipped to handle the risks of that kind of ministry."

From the very beginning, churches have implemented wise strategies to protect themselves from those who'd exploit their generosity. In fact, we find in the New Testament a policy statement Paul had written for the church in Ephesus, to guide their benevolence program for widows. (See 1 Timothy 5:3-15.) It's a fascinating passage which exemplifies both love and discernment.

Again, mature Christlike love sees human nature as it really is. Naive idealism will not survive the harsh realities of this world. That's why Jesus tells us to blend our compassion with generous amounts of wisdom.

Love Does Not Guarantee Everyone Will Like You

Misguided idealism can lead to another misconception that goes something like this: "If I show true love in all my relationships, then everyone will like me, and we'll all share together in the warm fuzzy feelings." It's a compelling vision but flawed for one notable reason: The most loving person in history was Jesus Christ, but a lot of people hated him in return—so much so, they had him crucified. And if the world hated Jesus, we are told, it will hate those who follow him (John 15:19).

Certainly, as we grow in love, our relationships in general will improve dramatically. After all, God's Spirit cultivates love, patience, and kindness within us, all virtues that harmonious relationships require. But even perfect love is no guarantee all our relationships will be easy. After all, Scripture reminds us to be patient with one another. Patience basically means kindly put up with the irksome imperfections of your neighbor. So, while love might increase the frequency of warm fuzzy feelings in our relationships, we'll have to persevere through a lot of cold, prickly moments as well.

Please don't miss it: Nowhere has God promised that everyone will like you or appreciate your devotion to the Golden Rule. Many will. But many will not. In fact, Jesus expected many would not. "Love your enemies," he says. "Do what is good to those who hate you, bless those who curse you, pray for those who mistreat you." (Luke 6:27-28, HCSB) So, clearly, there are circumstances when love has little to do with warm fuzzy feelings. Instead, it's the gutsy and painful decision to serve the one who least deserves it.

All this is leading us toward a truth that is daunting as it is magnificent: God is calling us to love those who are the most difficult to love, even making ourselves vulnerable to injury. Again,

> *God is calling us to love those who are the most difficult to love,*
> *even making ourselves vulnerable to injury.*

I fear many Christians have not fully absorbed the true nature of Christlike love, and that leads to disillusionment as seen in this common scenario: A Christian reaches out to someone in love—only to get wounded in return. And stinging from the injury, he wonders, *What did I do wrong? Why didn't they appreciate what I did?* And he becomes deeply discouraged. He even considers leaving the church altogether, determined never to be hurt again.

May I suggest something a little shocking? When you try to love someone and get wounded in return, you should welcome the injury as a badge of honor, really, as a gift from the Lord. You see, when God brings that difficult person into your life, he has invited you to aspire to the highest glory of all—to love others as Christ has loved you. And that means welcoming the injuries that will inevitably come.

Do I have your attention? Then I invite you to keep reading.

Chapter 12

A Wounded Love

As we have seen, the command to "Love your neighbor as yourself" serves as a gateway to breathtaking glory. No man is a failure who loves. And yet there remains a pathway that leads even higher, toward even greater glory, and it all begins with these words Jesus said to his disciples: "I give you a new command: Love one another. Just as I have loved you, you must also love one another." (John 13:34, HCSB)

Notice how Jesus' words convey something old and something new. We see the age-old command to love. But we also see an invitation to a new and higher standard: *Love as I have loved you.* So, what does it mean to love as Jesus loved? Admittedly, the answer would fill an entire library, but for the moment, I want to examine one aspect of Jesus' love which we broached in the last chapter: Jesus' love is a wounded love. To put it another way, love requires us to be vulnerable, to risk being injured. And if we're willing to accept it, there is heavenly glory in the pain.

Difficult People

Some people are easy to love. Personally, God has blessed me with many Christian friends who respond to my kindness with appreciation. They show love right back to me, they are alert to my needs, and they encourage my faith in the Lord. I rejoice in those relationships, and I know God rejoices as well because he longs for his family to dwell together in harmony (Psalm 133). I hope you can say the same about your own circle of friends.

When it comes to measuring the maturity of my love, however, I must look beyond the easy relationships. I need to ask myself—*honestly* ask myself—how am I doing at loving the *difficult* people in my life? Consider what Jesus says on the matter.

> Love your enemies and pray for those who persecute you, so that you may be sons of your Father in heaven. For He causes His sun to rise on the evil and the good, and sends rain on the righteous and the unrighteous. For if you love those who love you, what reward will you have? Don't even the tax collectors do the same? And if you greet only your brothers, what are you doing out of the ordinary? Don't even the Gentiles do the same? Be perfect, therefore, as your heavenly Father is perfect.

(Jesus, Matthew 5:44-48, HCSB)

What Jesus says is plainly true yet often overlooked: Loving our friends is not much trouble. Even the godless know how to do that. But if we aspire to embody God's kind of love, we must go beyond friendly territory and risk injury that comes from loving the annoying, the inconsiderate, the hurtful, and the selfish.

As Jesus reminds us in the passage above, our Heavenly Father has chosen to love the undeserving. He provides the sunrise for the sinners as well as the saints. He sends the rain to the thankless as well as the grateful. It's only fitting that we, his followers, love in like manner. When we choose to love those who least deserve it, we become sons of our Father in heaven, says Jesus. In other words, we become the spitting image of the God we serve.

Every fiber of our earthly being protests this kind of love. Personally, I can muster a dozen excuses why Jesus' command to love the unlovable should not apply to my situation. But none of my arguments can withstand this simple question: If God had chosen to withhold his love from difficult people, where would that leave me? And, if you don't mind me asking, where would that leave you? How difficult was it for God to love us?

To find the answer, I suggest we go on a long walk together, back to the cross of Christ. It's not enough to stand far away at a safe distance; we must press closer and closer to Golgotha until we recoil at what the Son of God has become on our behalf, a wreckage of flesh and blood. "His appearance was so disfigured that He did not look like a man," wrote the prophet Isaiah, "and His form did not resemble a human being." (Isaiah 52:14, HCSB)

We need to sense, as well, how vastly alone Jesus was on the cross. Most of his friends had abandoned him. There were no voices of comfort, only insults from the crowd of mockers. "He saved others, but he cannot save Himself!" For a time, he even felt abandoned by his Heavenly Father, "My God, my God, why have you forsaken me?"

As we kneel at the foot of the cross, where the soil is tacky with his blood, we need to remember whose sins Jesus was paying for. It was not for his own sin. He committed no sin. It was for my sin. And for yours. "For God so loved the world," goes the familiar verse, "that he gave his only begotten Son." Only at the cross do we understand what those words required of our Lord. To say we were difficult to love is the understatement of the ages.

I'll be honest. When God chose to love me to the point of blood, sweat, and tears, I was not a trophy catch for the kingdom. I was one of those difficult people. I was annoying, I was hurtful, I was selfish, and I was cruel. That's why, if I'm serious about loving as Jesus loves, I must look beyond the easy relationships and ask how I'm doing with the hard relationships—loving those people who question my motives, who cut me down, who take my sacrifices for granted, who lie to me, who lie about me, who disappoint me.

I've known quite a few Christians who have walked away from the church because, as they put it, "I've been hurt!" Or they've been sitting out of ministry because, "I've been hurt!" Or they've promised never to help anyone again because, "I've been hurt!" Their injuries are varied and legion: "No one ever came to visit me." "I never heard a thank-you for all I'd done." "I was stabbed in the back." Or "They broke their promise."

The list of grievances could go on forever, but sooner or later we must come to terms with an obvious fact: You are not the first to have been hurt by the church, nor am I. We tend to forget that our savior was hurt by the church of his day. It was men of the cloth who conspired to have him crucified. If that's not reason enough for Jesus to give up on the church, I don't know what is.

The reason we call God's love not just grace, but *amazing* grace, is because he continued to love us even after we gave him every reason to walk away. Jesus paid the highest price when we were at our worst. It was in the valley of deepest hurt that we see the grandeur of his love. And this same Jesus says to us, "Love one another as I have loved you."

From Bitterness to Praise

How many among us are nursing old wounds? Is it time to stop reminding anyone who'll listen "how badly those people hurt me?" God calls us to an altogether different way of thinking: Our wounds are cause for praise. Our Heavenly Father has granted us the glorious privilege of being wounded for love, as Jesus was.

The apostle Peter, with a tender heart, reminds us, "God called you to do good, even if it means suffering, just as Christ suffered for you. He is your example, and you must follow in his steps." (1 Peter 2:21, NLT) Please don't miss the import of Peter's words: Whatever road of suffering you've traveled, look around; you'll find Jesus' footsteps have gone before you.

Have you been insulted? Jesus was mocked while dying on a cross (Matthew 27:40-41).

Are you the victim of unfair criticism? The religious leaders accused Jesus of ministering in the power of Satan (Matthew 12:24).

Does no one understand you? Well, did anyone truly understand Jesus? Recall his poignant appeal to Philip in the upper room: "Have I been with you all this time, Philip, and yet you still don't know who I am?" (John 14:9, NLT)

Have your friends let you down? During Jesus' darkest hour, his friends "deserted Him and ran away." (Mark 14:50, HCSB)

Were you betrayed? Remember Judas (Matthew 26:14-16).

Were you humiliated? Soldiers stripped Jesus of his clothes, made a spectacle of him, and forced him to carry his cross through the streets, enduring the howls and jeers of the public (Matthew 27:27-31).

Is the stubbornness of people testing your patience? "You unbelieving and rebellious generation!" Jesus said one day. "How long will I be with you? How long must I put up with you?" (Matthew 17:17, HCSB)

Has your family turned on you? Jesus' own family tried to restrain him, thinking he was out of His mind (Mark 3:21).

Again, our Heavenly Father calls us to endure only what Jesus our savior has already endured on our behalf, without complaint. "He did not retaliate when he was insulted, nor threaten revenge when he suffered. He left his case in the hands of God, who always judges fairly." (1 Peter 2:23, NLT)

Mark those words. Jesus took that natural longing for payback and surrendered it to his Heavenly Father. All the terrible injustices he endured, he entrusted them to the one who has promised, "Vengeance is mine, I will repay." (Romans 12:19, NASB) By letting go of the sword, Jesus was free to love.

Is it time for some of you to let go of the sword? Yes, what those people did to you was wrong, and you're still bleeding from the wounds. But why not, as Jesus did, surrender the sword of vengeance to your Heavenly Father? Put your case in the hands of God who always judges fairly. Let him mete out judgment on your behalf when the time is right. In the meantime, *your* hands will be free to serve and to love.

Yes, you will have to live with the consequences of other people's sins, but didn't Jesus, out of love, bear the consequences of *your* sin? "He personally carried our sins in his body on the cross ... By his wounds you are healed." (1 Peter 2:24, NLT)

All of us should become reacquainted with a man who embraced these truths with shocking enthusiasm, namely, Paul the apostle. Describing the demands of his missionary work, he wrote, "Up to the present hour, we are both hungry and thirsty; we are poorly clothed, roughly treated, homeless; we labor, working with our own hands. When we are reviled, we bless; when we are persecuted, we endure it; when we are slandered, we respond graciously. Even now, we are like the world's garbage, like the dirt everyone scrapes off their sandals." (1 Corinthians 4:11-13, HCSB)

Ouch! *I'm treated like the dirt people scrape off their sandals?!* Have the hardships of ministry turned Paul into a cynic? Not all! For he also writes, "I am glad when I suffer for you in my body, for I am participating in the sufferings of Christ that continue for his body, the church." (Colossians 1:24, NLT) Here, then, was Paul's perspective: *Jesus suffered for the good of the church, and in every way possible, I want to be like Jesus.*

Perhaps you should bookmark this chapter for future reference because it's inevitable: As you aspire to grow in love, eventually someone will hurt you in return. At that moment, when you're dealing with the sting of being injured, you have a choice: You can turn inward and become bitter. Or you can look to your Heavenly Father and thank him for inviting you toward the highest glory of all, to love others as Christ has loved us. That means loving those who are difficult to love, who least deserve our love. And it means bearing their wounds without complaint.

"I give you a new command," says Jesus. "Love one another. Just as I have loved you, you must also love one another." What an honor, to embody his love in a world that badly needs his amazing grace.

Part 5
Glory on the Job

Work willingly at whatever you do,
as though you were working for the Lord rather than for people.
Remember that the Lord will give you an inheritance as your reward,
and that the Master you are serving is Christ.

-Colossians 3:23-24
(NLT)

Chapter 13

Tied Down or Freed Up?

Let's talk about our jobs, shall we?

In the workplace, we find a lot of ordinary and not much glory, or so it seems. Whether you work in an office, in a shop, on a construction site, or in the home as a full-time mom, our vocation can be a source of chronic frustration. Work responsibilities demand huge chunks of our time and emotional energy, which is especially frustrating for those who want to be more involved in serving the Lord. Our co-workers drag us down spiritually. Our bosses can be hard to please. The days are stress-filled. The complaints are endless.

When we read the New Testament, we find that job frustration is nothing new. The first generation of Christians struggled to find meaning in the daily grind just as we do. In fact, Christians in the first century had it a lot worse for one simple reason: Many among them were slaves!

Slavery pervaded the first-century Roman Empire just as it had every society since the beginning of time. In some locales, slaves comprised a majority of the population. As you can imagine, a slave who became a Christian might grow discontent with his "work situation," longing for the freedom to serve the Lord unhindered. Legally, however, a slave was someone else's property, so he couldn't simply hand in his two-weeks' notice. These brothers and sisters in Christ needed real encouragement, and the apostles rose to the occasion. Their hope-filled messages to the slave, preserved in pages of the New Testament, speak with amazing relevance even today.

(Note: Some in my reading audience might have questions about how the Bible handles the topic of slavery, so I have included a short article in the appendix to address that concern. If you're feeling at all uncomfortable about this section, I encourage you to turn to page 227. Then resume this chapter afterward.)

It's surprising but true: Today's employee has more in common with the first-century slave than many realize. For one thing, slaves performed all kinds of jobs, from blue-collar to white-collar work, skilled and unskilled alike. Some performed menial tasks while others held great responsibility managing homes or business enterprises. In fact, point to any vocation today, and you can find a counterpart performed by a slave in the first century.

Bosses and slave masters have a few things in common as well. Some masters were fair and respectful to their slaves; others were a terror. It's the same with bosses today. Granted, a modern employee can quit his job to escape an exploitive boss, but it's not always a realistic option. If the worker can't afford the financial risk of leaving, he's stuck. "The company owns me," complains the worker. "My boss is a slave-driver!"

So, when it comes to vocational frustration, today's Christian and his first-century brother are not so far apart after all, and that's why the passages in the Bible written to slaves continue to speak with amazing relevance. Below is one such message from Paul. If you fear your job stands in the way of serving the Lord, what you are about to read is going to blow your mind.

Each person should remain in the life situation in which he was called. Were you called while a slave? It should not be a concern to you. But if you can become free, by all means take the opportunity. For he who is called by the Lord as a slave is the Lord's freedman. Likewise he who is called as a free man is Christ's slave. You were bought at a price; do not become slaves of men. Brothers, each person should remain with God in whatever situation he was called.

(1 Corinthians 7:20-24, HCSB)

Amazing. According to Paul, the Christian slave is entirely free to live for the Lord. He is the Lord's freedman after all. This is powerful truth. If the slave is completely free to live for Christ, how much more is today's employee who feels held back by his responsibilities at work?

To underscore the point, Paul offers this word of caution: "You were bought at a price; do not become slaves of men." Ultimately, Christ is the one who owns you—body, mind, and spirit—for all eternity because he purchased you with his blood. So, you should never define your life based on who your earthly master (or boss) is; otherwise, you have become enslaved to a mere mortal. No earthly master (or boss) owns you. Christ owns you. For that reason alone, no mere human can limit God's promises and plans for your life. Period. Please, don't miss this:

No human being, including your employer,
Has the power to limit God's promises and plans for your life.

Whether you are a slave or a hired worker, in Christ you are "the Lord's freedman." You are free to serve God right where you are. Paul was so confident of this, he wrote, "Each person should remain in the life situation in which he was called." In other words, now that you are a Christian, there is no need to make a sudden career change. God will use you right where you are. There is glory-potential in your ordinary job.

At this point, a word of clarification is in order. Some Bible students have concluded, based on the passage above, that a Christian is required to stick with his current job forever. They cite verse 24 as support, "Brothers, each person should remain with God in whatever situation he was called." That conclusion is misguided, however, because Paul, in the very same passage, also writes, "But if you can become free, by all means take the opportunity." In other words, Paul had no problem with a Christian leaving slavery if he could do so legally. But he wanted everyone to understand that their status, whether slave or free, in no way limits their potential to serve the Lord.

So then, God has not bound you to your current job forever. (Aren't you glad?) You are free to leave if you wish. But before you make any rash decisions, I urge you to keep reading. It's important you learn to invite heaven's glory into the workplace, whether it's the job you have now or the one you hope to have in the future.

Meet Your New Boss

Again, no human being, including your employer, has the power to limit God's promises and plans for your life. Now, here is where things get wonderfully practical. In his letter to the Colossians, Paul shows us how to transform our daily work into something sacred in God's eyes. To help us see its relevance to the modern workplace, I have tweaked the passage slightly, converting the ancient slave-terminology to modern job-terminology. The result is profound:

Brothers and sisters in the Lord, when you are on the job, obey your earthly boss in everything you do. Try to please him all the time, not just when he is watching you. Serve him sincerely because of your reverent fear of the Lord. Work willingly at whatever you do, as though you were working for the Lord rather than for people. Remember that the Lord will give you an inheritance as your reward, and that the Boss you are really serving is Christ. But if you do what is wrong (like padding your timesheet or stealing office supplies), you will be paid back for the wrong you have done. For God has no favorites.

(Adapted from Colossians 3:22-25, NLT)

Please notice: Your performance on the job is near and dear to God's heart, so much so Paul drops this bombshell: "The Boss [literally *the Master*] you are serving is Christ." That is simply stunning. If you show up to work each day reporting to that "miserable boss" who owns the company, you have set your sights far too low. Never forget that you answer to a higher boss—the Lord Jesus Christ. A friend of mine, before he retired, displayed a small sign in his office, "My Boss is a Jewish Carpenter," a clever reminder who he really served.

According to Paul, when you approach your work as an assignment from God, "the Lord will give you an inheritance as a reward." The reward here transcends a mere raise or promotion. Paul's terminology points to an eternal inheritance—riches in God's eternal kingdom that you will enjoy forever. Wow, this is simply profound, and it's a huge encouragement for the Christian who is convinced his job is a barrier to achieving eternal glory.

All of this raises a question: Why in the world do we call our non-church jobs secular work?! Does God view our jobs as just secular work? Obviously not, based on what we see in Scripture. The next time we show up at our workplace, perhaps we should remove our shoes. Like Moses, it seems we're treading on holy ground.

Okay, back to our passage where the blessings continue. Paul goes on, **"Obey your earthly [boss] in everything you do..."** Because your boss occupies a place of authority, you must treat him with appropriate respect and follow his lead. Authority structures are not some human invention; God is the one who established them (Romans 13:1-2). The person in authority sets the direction for the company, the department, or whatever group he is tasked to lead. If there is a tough decision to be made and there is no consensus, the one in authority has the right to cast the final decision. It's all a part of God's design.

Many readers, I suspect, want to object at this point. "You don't know my boss! How can I possibly respect his leadership?!" The truth is, respecting authority demands a lot from us. It requires humility, maturity, and wise judgment—especially when our boss makes terrible decisions, has unreasonable expectations, or pressures us to do something unethical. There's no doubt about it: Respecting authority in a way that is godly and wise poses a huge challenge. Just ask some of the great men of God who served under bad leadership: David served King Saul, Elijah served King Ahab, and Daniel served King Nebuchadnezzar. (You'll find their biographies in First Samuel, First Kings, and the book of Daniel, respectively.)

So, we have a decision to make. Many Christians, sadly, will shrug off what God has clearly said and go back to "sticking it to the man" in lockstep with the rest of the world. Others, the rare breed, will recognize the great opportunity God has handed them. He's given them a noble but difficult task of respecting human authority while remaining loyal to God. They will give it their best, trusting God will guide their steps. They'll endure frustration, setbacks, and tough lessons, but that's the price of godly maturity. We don't become our best when things are easy; our faith and our character grow best under pressure. That's how we become the David or the Elijah or the Daniel in our corner of the world.

"Try to please [your boss] all the time, not just when he is watching you. Serve him sincerely." The world at large tends to respect authority only to the degree it benefits them. When the boss is not looking, they revert to their self-serving ways. Do not follow their examples. Demonstrate trustworthy character even when the boss is out for the day. Do not be the guy who sponges from the company every perk and benefit he can get, ethically or otherwise. Be the guy who goes above and beyond the call of duty. Keep a clear conscience. God watches and remembers.

So there it is. Paul's charge to the worker, whether slave or free, comprises only a short paragraph, but it's packed with a lifetime of opportunity. And therein lies the glory—when we see our jobs as a God-assigned mission and approach our work with a devotion worthy of his majesty.

Once again, something that looks so ordinary on the surface is packed with amazing glory just waiting to be revealed. That's the transforming power of Jesus Christ. And we're just getting started.

Chapter 14

Rediscovering
the Goodness of Work

Because our jobs can be a source of so much stress, we tend to forget that work is actually a good thing. (No, that wasn't a typo. Work is a *good* thing.) God himself is a worker. He poured his strength and imagination into creating the universe as its divine architect, artist, and engineer. When it was all completed, he said with deep satisfaction, "It is *very* good" (Genesis 1:31). Because God created us in his own image, we long for meaningful work. That's why a life of idleness destroys the human spirit.

All of us, at one time or another, have experienced the exhilaration of pouring ourselves into a project that brought us pleasure. Perhaps it was a garden you cultivated, a car you restored, a broken appliance you repaired, a picture you sketched, a room you repainted, or a computer you built from spare parts. Afterward, you stepped back, smiled at the finished product, and thought to yourself, "It is good." At that moment you experienced a bit of the pleasure God felt when he created the heavens and the earth. It's all a part of being made in his image.

Yes, work is a good thing, and it's important we don't lose sight of that. In this chapter, we'll identify the lies and half-truths that distort our view of work. Our vocations are challenging enough without adding discouraging falsehoods to the mix. I pray this chapter will bring our vocations into proper perspective and help us see, with fresh eyes, the goodness and the glory of a job well-done.

"It is Good."

The first falsehood is a biggie: Some Christians believe that work is the consequence of Adam's sin, a form of punishment from God. But that's not true. Adam and Eve were gardeners by vocation prior to their fall into sin (Genesis 2:15). From the beginning, God intended for humankind to experience the gratification of fruitful labor. So, work is not only a good thing; it's a God-thing.

The problem is not the work. The problem is the curse God placed on work in response to Adam's sin. The curse has altered work in two major ways: Work became frustrating, and work became an economic necessity. We find these two dynamics in God's pronouncement against Adam, "The ground is cursed because of you. You will eat from it by means of painful labor all the days of your life." (3:17, HCSB)

From that day forward, if Adam wanted to eat, he had to get up and go to work. He no longer had access to the free buffet in the Garden of Eden (2:8-9). Adam would punch the clock every morning for the rest of his life. It was work or starve. And much of his job experience would be summed up in two words, "painful labor." We still live with that curse today. Why is work so stressful at times? It's the curse of "painful labor" going all the way back to Adam. And why do we stick with our stressful, frustrating job? Because, just like Adam, it's work or starve.

Here's the point. We were made to work. Work is a good thing. Adam's sin and the ensuing consequences are what transformed fulfilling labor into *frustration* and *painful labor*. As we seek to handle the stress of work with Godly wisdom, we must learn to appreciate the goodness of work itself. Work is God's idea. And on our best days, we experience his pleasure in what we do.

Years ago, I discovered a powerful discipline that helps me see the glory in my work every day, a nugget of wisdom I discovered when watching the video curriculum based on Pastor John Ortberg's book *The Life You Always Wanted.* The author takes us back to the days of creation and reminds us how, at the close of each day, God looked over his work and said, "It is good." Pastor Ortberg recommends we develop a similar rhythm in our daily work. We should work for a while and then step back and take pleasure in what we have accomplished.

When I worked as a field technician for several years, I installed equipment in the basement-level departments of hospitals. During the installation, things tended to get messy: Wires were poking from junction boxes, components and tools were scattered throughout the department, and ceiling tiles were askew. After a couple of days, once the job was completed, the department was tidy again, and all the newly installed equipment looked great. My final walk-around was a sweet experience. I usually worked alone, so it was just the Lord and me taking that tour together. I enjoyed those "It-is-good moments." The habit helped me see the nobility in my work.

Let me ask you, do you take time to admire your own handiwork? You should. Next time, instead of hurrying off to the next task, stop and behold what you have accomplished. After you've finished cleaning house, walk around and admire how nice the place looks. When you hear the hum of the engine you repaired, smile with the pride of a professional. Behold the wall you painted, the floor you mopped, the lesson you taught—and say to yourself, "You know, this is good. I'm pleased." In time, your eyes will open wide to the glory of even the smallest task, and that's when you experience the deep-down pleasure of our Creator who long, long ago said to himself, "It is good."

God's Gym

When we go through tough times, God's promises in Scripture become a source of profound encouragement. One promise often quoted is Romans 8:28, "We know that all things work together for the good of those who love God: those who are called according to His purpose." (HCSB) Think of it: Whatever our circumstances, we can say with confidence, "God is in this. He is using it to further his good plan in my life."

Unfortunately, there seems to be one major exception to the 8:28 promise: our jobs. Given the level of despair among Christians in the workplace, it seems God isn't up to the challenge. "My job situation is so messed up," we cry, "even God doesn't know what to do with it!" So, the promise of the abundant life remains stifled "all because of my dumb job!"

Bummer.

Okay, time to get real. Why are we so apt to believe our job is the one thing standing between us and God's will for our lives? Have we forgotten that God is so rich with love and vast in power, that he oversees all the complex interactions of earthly events to bring his plans to fruition? "Because we are united with Christ," writes Paul, "we have received an inheritance from God, for he chose us in advance, and *he makes everything work out according to his plan.*" (Ephesians 1:11, NLT)

Is it time for some of us to admit, deep down, we've lost faith in God's ability to use our jobs to accomplish his good and perfect will in our lives? Is it time to cast ourselves upon the promise of Romans

8:28 all over again, even though we've heard it quoted a million times?

> We know that **all things** work together for the good of those who love God: those who are called according to His purpose. For those He foreknew He also predestined **to be conformed to the image of His Son**, so that He would be the firstborn among many brothers.

(Romans 8:28-29, HCSB)

Let's look at those verses with fresh eyes. What do we see? First, God is always working for our good, that is, for our best and highest interests. Second, what is the "good" God is aiming for? He is transforming our character to resemble that of his son Jesus Christ. Third, what circumstances does God use toward that end? *All* circumstances, including our jobs.

In fact, I suggest the workplace serves as one of the most effective gymnasiums for character conditioning. It is the perfect laboratory to develop perseverance, to gain practical wisdom, to train you how to handle stress, and to teach you to set priorities. It's a great environment to polish your people skills and to build relationships with those who don't know God. The possibilities are endless.

All of this assumes one thing, of course—that you are all-in on God's plan. You must be fully invested in the Lord's strategy to mold you into a man or a woman whose love, character, and faith resemble that of the Lord Jesus Christ.

Do you know why the workplace is such an excellent training facility? Because it's difficult. It's hard. It's painful. It's grueling. And that's how we grow, as Paul explains:

We can rejoice, too, when we run into ***problems and trials,*** for we know that ***they help us develop endurance.*** And endurance develops ***strength of character***, and character strengthens our confident hope of salvation. And this hope will not lead to disappointment. ***For we know how dearly God loves us, because he has given us the Holy Spirit to fill our hearts with his love.***

(Romans 5:3-5, NLT)

Notice the link between stressful circumstances ("problems and trials") and the opportunity to develop godly character ("endurance … strength of character"). Like any concerned father, God is committed to our future. With perfect love, he is shaping us to become more like Christ. God loves us too much to let us settle for the cheap stuff in life.

Also, in the passage quoted above, make sure you catch that last sentence, the one that reminds us how God "has given us the Holy Spirit to fill our hearts with his love." Our Heavenly Father is not a drill-sergeant wannabe who enjoys inflicting pain. His love is perfect, and he really does have our best interests at heart, even when he's leading us through difficult circumstances.

Here's a practical way to think about all this. The stress you experience at work and your reaction to it is God's way of helping you identify where your character needs to grow. Are you resorting to white lies and half-truths to get through the day? Then you need to grow in honesty. Are you struggling to stay composed when the challenges multiply? Then you have the opportunity to develop inner peace and courage. Are you frustrated because people walk all over you like a doormat? Then you need to learn how to be assertive—the godly kind of assertiveness that speaks plainly while maintaining gentleness and courtesy. Are you blowing up at people? Then you must learn patience.

In talking with other Christians, I've concluded that work-stress is one of the hardest battlefields we deal with, especially among men. When work weighs a man down, it casts a pall on everything. That's when we must band together as brothers in Christ and help each other stay strong.

May I offer some heartfelt counsel to those of you struggling with job-stress? First, kneel before God and tell him exactly what's on your heart. Hold nothing back. Perhaps you need to confess that, yes, you've doubted his goodness for a long time. You've bought into the lie that your work situation is too big for him to handle. Confess and ask for his forgiveness. He will not turn you away. A broken and contrite heart opens the door to God's compassion (Psalm 51:17).

Second, band together with others of like mind and pray for each other. Men, find other God-loving men. Women, find other God-loving women. As you pray, claim Romans 8:28 again and again, believing with confidence that nothing in your life is an accident. God, even at this very moment, is working to fulfill his plan for your life. Ask him for a spiritual breakthrough, that you'd develop the kind of character that handles adversity in a Christlike manner.

Finally, immerse yourself in the book of Proverbs. Let it become a lifelong friend. You'll discover it's filled with practical wisdom that has amazing relevance to your responsibilities at work. In my own life, Proverbs has been a mentoring-like influence, giving me insight into what true character and integrity look like.

Oh, and one more thing. Be sure to thank your Heavenly Father—really thank him—for this chance to mature as a follower of Christ. He loves you very much and wants you to achieve all the glory you possibly can.

Stay on the Front Lines!

One pernicious lie that poisons the attitude of Christians toward their job is this: They're convinced the demands of work prevent them from doing "real kingdom ministry." "I have no time to serve the Lord," they say, and they look with envy to the full-time ministers—the pastors, youth leaders, and missionaries—because "that's where the real action is."

Do you know what's funny? I used to be one of those guys in full-time ministry, serving as a pastor for over a decade, and I grew envious of those who had normal jobs outside the walls of the church. You see, I was convinced those with "non-ministry jobs" were on the front lines of God's work, rubbing shoulders with those who don't know Christ.

Here was my frustration: Pastors, generally speaking, are cut off from the outside world. It's the nature of the work. We spend most of our time preaching to the choir, that is, interacting with members of our congregation who already know the Lord. And those in the pews who don't know the Lord have heard the Gospel message *ad nauseum* from the pulpit. After serving as pastor for a while, I felt frustrated because I had few opportunities to connect with people who didn't know Christ.

Even when I got away from the church to rub elbows with non-Christians, the barriers went up as soon as people discovered I was a pastor. I was no longer a normal guy in their eyes. When someone asked what I did for a living, I knew the conversation was about to hit a major pothole. "A pastor? That's interesting. Gee, look at the time. I should be going." I was the perfect conversation killer. Yes, there were days I longed to be just Tim and not Pastor Tim.

The truth is, those in full-time ministry and those in the civilian workplace don't need to be envious of each other. We just need to see the strategic value of our God-given assignment. Each role is vital to kingdom work. If you're convinced the grass is greener on the other side, be careful lest you miss the opportunities right in front of you.

To all of you with "regular jobs," the kingdom needs you right where you are. Unless your boss sponsors a Bring-Your-Pastor-to-Work Day, who else is better suited to serve as kingdom ambassador? The truth is, even if your boss did sponsor a Bring-Your-Pastor-to-Work Day, you are still the most effective ambassador for the kingdom—by far! Your example on the job is much more powerful than any pastor's. You see, everyone expects a pastor to be well-behaved. After all, it's his job to be godly, right? But when people watch you, the non-pastor person, living a godly life, it's harder for them to dismiss your behavior.

Good Christian character in the workplace stands out. It compels people to wonder, *Why do I never hear you use profanity? How come you never engage in the backstabbing gossip that goes on around here? Why don't you traffic in the white lies like everybody else? How come you don't gripe and complain? How come you're the only person I know who admits to making a mistake and actually apologizes for it? You have such a kind heart. Why is that?*

See? You can powerfully demonstrate that the Gospel of Jesus Christ is more than an interesting story pastors talk about on Sunday morning. Your day-to-day living shows that Jesus Christ is real and dynamic, that Christianity is for life in the real world, not just an hour on Sunday. Again, you are the word of God made flesh in your corner of the kingdom.

At this point, some of you are growing uncomfortable because you suspect I'm about to talk about the "e-word:" evangelism, in the workplace of all things! Listen, I feel your pain. The idea of being an evangelist on the job makes a lot of us feel uncomfortable, if not a little nauseous. The problem, I believe, is that many of us have inherited an approach to evangelism that makes everyone involved feel weirded out.

Some evangelism strategies pressure us to behave like a bachelor who's desperate to get married but has no patience for dating. He's the guy who blurts on every first date, "Will you marry me?" While he deserves high marks for boldness, the poor girl is left shell-shocked. Chances are, there will be no *second* date. Unfortunately, that's how many of us have learned to do evangelism: No thoughtfulness. No sensitivity. Just barge right in and close the deal.

Don't get me wrong. God uses bold evangelists. I've met people who have a God-given gift for winning others to Christ in extraordinary ways. They charge in where angels fear to tread. When I meet a bold evangelist, the best thing I can do is get out of his way. My cautious temperament will only slow him down. I say to all bold evangelists, "God bless you, and may your tribe increase!"

Most of us, though, don't have the gifts for bold evangelism. That's okay. God distributes gifts to the body of Christ as he sees fit (1 Corinthians 12:7). But all of us can still be a powerful influence for Christ. We simply need to play to our strengths, mindful of how God has wired us to serve.

Here's my advice. Don't feel pressured to close the deal when it comes to evangelism. Focus on being a good neighbor as we learned earlier. Evangelism often requires a period of courtship, if you will. Building trust with others takes time. Your coworkers want to know if your kindness toward them is authentic, or are you one more boy scout working on his evangelism merit badge? Don't view people as spiritual projects. People can smell that a mile away. Love them as God loves them, with a heart that is pure and full of genuine compassion. Meanwhile, pray for them—really pray for them—and ask God to open the door in his time.

Be patient. Be thoughtful. And be wise.

A great way to break the ice regarding your faith is to have something displayed on your desk or in your workspace that lets people know God is important to you, perhaps an ornament with a

Bible verse or a God-centered quote. Be tasteful, of course. Don't be "that guy" on the highway whose car is plastered with hundreds of bumper stickers. The idea is to draw people in, not scare them away. Be inviting, not condemning. When someone asks about it, tell a little bit of your story.

When I had an office job, I looked for opportunities to talk about my church family. Monday morning, when someone asked what I did over the weekend, I'd mention that our family went to church. Occasionally I'd do a little bragging about my Christian friends. I might share a bit of sage advice I learned from "one of the guys in our men's group." I want people to see that church is not a religious institution. It's a vibrant fellowship where people have been transformed by God's love.

Over time, my coworkers learned a few important facts about me: A) I'm not a religious freak, B) My relationship with God was important to me, and C) I treated people with kindness. That, in turn, opened doors into people's lives. As those relationships matured, coworkers began to confide in me about their struggles, sometimes work-related, sometimes family-related. They knew I was a considerate listener and would respect their privacy.

During some of those closed-door conversations, when I sensed the time was right, I even asked my coworker if I could pray for him. If he said okay, I'd bow my head and offer a short, compassionate prayer, right there in his office. It was a great way for people to learn that I'm not into religion. Rather, I'm all about serving a God who is *real, personal, and compassionate.*

That's my story. Trust me; I'm not a perfect evangelist. I struggle like you do. But it's an exciting adventure, wouldn't you agree? Take the advice I've given and use what's helpful. In the end, you have your own God-given way of relating to people. Embrace it. The Lord wants to write a story through you, a story that is uniquely yours.

So, will you be God's ambassador right where you are? Be patient with the process. Often, when the Lord is leading someone toward salvation, it requires a long journey from the darkness toward the light. The Lord might use your influence to nudge someone a little further along the path. Then, in the future, the Lord will raise up a servant to close the deal. As Jesus said, both the sower and the reaper will rejoice in the harvest (John 4:36).

If I was pastor all over again, this is what I'd say to my congregation: "We are a team. If we embrace our assigned roles, God will work through us to help people find their way to Jesus. You serve as the light of Christ in places I can never reach. That's why your presence in the workplace and the community is vital. Be God's light in the world. Pray for your coworkers. Love them as Christ loves you. And when the time comes, if you need help closing the deal, invite them to church. That gives me, your pastor, the opportunity to use the gifts God has given me. I promise to provide a worship service where you feel comfortable bringing your friends, a safe place for him to learn about Jesus."

Believe me, your influence on the job is vital to kingdom work. You are God's soldier on the frontline, shining the light of Christ in places your pastor could never go. Be the presence of Christ on the job. The kingdom needs you right where you are.

Part 6
The Glory of Family

*Didn't the L*ORD *make you one with your wife?*
In body and spirit you are his.
And what does he want? Godly children from your union.
So guard your heart; remain loyal to the wife of your youth.

-Malachi 2:15
(NLT)

Chapter 15
Family:
Recovering the Glory

The more we understand God's ways, the more we discover heavenly glory is closer than we ever imagined. In fact, we are about to uncover vast potential right in our own homes. You see, the day you became a husband or a wife, a father or a mother, God bestowed upon you an awesome responsibility to love, nurture, and care for a family dearly precious to him. The problem is, if your house is like ours, all that heavenly glory is buried under seven piles of laundry.

Let's be honest. While family life is full of wonderful blessings, it's also hard work. Maintaining a healthy marriage is challenging. Raising kids is exhausting. And the never-ending demands can overwhelm us: late nights with crying babies, words spoken in anger, endless carpooling to games and events, tough conversations, parenting mistakes, piles of laundry, forgotten anniversaries, tantrums, stress with the in-laws, more parenting mistakes, drama queens, drama kings, heartbreak, misunderstandings, and more parenting mistakes, not to mention all that money flying out the window to pay for school, clothes, and activities.

And therein lies the challenge: We become so weary in our duties, we lose sight of the high privilege of leading a family, and then we are tempted to look elsewhere for glory. This is not a modern problem. It's as old as family itself. We find John the Baptist, two millennia ago, having to address the dissolution of the family. It was his God-given mission to "turn the hearts of fathers to their children and the hearts of children to their fathers." (Malachi 4:6, HCSB) He implored his generation to turn their hearts toward home.

Is that message needed any less today? Consider the following passage from the Psalms and how it serves as a shocking contrast to our modern view of family:

> Children are a gift from the LORD;
>   they are a reward from him
> Children born to a young man
>   are like arrows in a warrior's hands.
> How joyful is the man whose quiver is full of them!
>
> (Psalm 127:3-5, NLT)

Is anyone out there praying for a quiver full of kids? If so, you are a dying breed. Comedian Jim Gaffigan, who is a father of five, said, "Big families are like waterbed stores. They used to be everywhere. Now they're just weird."

Listen, I'm not saying everyone needs to have big families. (Speaking personally, Megan and I love our three boys. If God gives us another, we'll take him and love him. But we aren't praying for one. We have our hands full!) Here's the point: If we aren't careful, we can let the toxic thinking in our culture poison our view of family. Instead of viewing home and family as blessings from the Lord, we regard them as entanglements which hinder us from pursuing the "really fun stuff" in life.

We need to get real about modern society's enlightened philosophy regarding family: It's nothing more than old-fashioned selfishness. Whether it's the radical feminist who views family as a form of slavery, the corporate leader who prioritizes business success over family success, or the guys at the bar hiding out from "the kids and the old lady," they are all driven by a desire to live for self. They know nothing of Jesus' call to lay down our lives for the good of others (1 John 3:16). And they know nothing of God's high calling to be a faithful mom or dad. But their philosophy has so permeated our society, it can poison our hearts and we hardly realize it.

When we surrender to the world's value system, it always ends in regret. It's a well-worn line but worth repeating: No one at the end of his life wished he had spent more time at the office. During our sunset years, we will see with special clarity what's most important in life. And these chapters on family are all about fixing our eyes on the hidden glory of home and family *right now* instead of waiting until it's too late. Yes, the glory is hidden much of the time. But God wants to open our eyes to the splendor, if we'll only listen to his voice.

Perspective

Out of all the chapters in this book, the ones on family have been the most daunting to write because few undertakings are as guilt-inducing as raising a family. Marriage and parenting will disclose the depths or the deficiencies of one's character like nothing else will. When I got married, I quickly realized God had thrown me into a crash-course on personal maturity. Early on, Megan and I couldn't even pick out a movie at the video store without making each other mad. And when our first child Levi was born, I was amazed how a little human being the size of a loaf of bread can undo thirty years of Christian sanctification in under an hour.

So, as I wax eloquent about the glory of family life, please rest assured that I am a work in progress just like you are. Those who write books, if we aren't careful, can come across as amazing experts who have life all figured out. That can be demoralizing to the reader. So, let me assure you, I have bad days just like you do. If I can string two good days in a row, I know I'm on a roll.

That's why, in these chapters on family, you'll find more inspiration than step-by-step instruction. Speaking personally, when I'm overwhelmed with the demands of being a husband and a father, an instruction manual reads like a guilt manual, a reminder of all the times I faltered. What I need most days is to catch a glimpse of the glory of being a good husband and a good father, something to keep me motivated during the tough times.

One final thought before we delve into family life. I have a special place in my heart for those who approach these chapters with fear and trembling. Perhaps you're learning these lessons too late. The days of raising a family are behind you, and you look back with regret because your marriage fell apart or your children have gone prodigal. Others of you are heartbroken because you did everything "by the book." You poured your heart, mind, and soul into your family, but for reasons that still don't make sense, it all crashed into the rocks. So much for the storybook life you imagined for yourself.

For those with broken hearts, a few words of encouragement: First, if these pages become too painful to read, go to your Heavenly Father and be honest about your heartbreak. Admit your failings. Be honest about your disappointments. Have a good cry in his arms. He wants to be near you in your pain. Remember, "He heals the brokenhearted and binds up their wounds." (Psalm 147:3 HCSB)

Now, take all that anguish and channel it toward earnest prayer for your family. King David, after a major failing, discovered prayer is especially powerful when it pours forth from a shattered life. "The sacrifice pleasing to God is a broken spirit," he prayed to the Lord, "...You will not despise a broken and humbled heart." (Psalm 51:17, HCSB) Indeed, genuine anguish gets God's attention.

And never forget, all through the ages the Lord has proven he knows how to build something beautiful out of our ruins. After the nation Israel failed terribly and suffered the consequences of their sin, the prophet Isaiah spoke these comforting words, "The Lord will always lead you, satisfy you in a parched land, and strengthen your bones ... Some of you will rebuild the ancient ruins; you will restore the foundations laid long ago; you will be called the repairer of broken walls, the restorer of streets where people live." (Isaiah 58:11-12, HCSB) Wrap these verses in your arms and carry them to God. Ask him to build something beautiful from the ruins in your life. He's done it before. He can do it again.

And rest assured, God knows how to accomplish his will even amidst the messiness of dysfunctional families. For inspiration, I suggest you read the biographies of Abraham, his son Isaac, and his grandson Jacob (Genesis chapters 12 to 50). You can't help but notice how much dysfunction plagued those three generations. And yet, despite all that messiness, God fulfilled his purposes through them.

So, for all of you living in the ruins of disappointment, I urge you to cast yourself onto the Lord. He knows how to bring back prodigals, and he knows how to build something beautiful out of all our broken pieces.

Chapter 16

Parenthood:

No Ordinary Moments

S o, are you ready to find glory beneath all those piles of laundry? Centuries ago the Lord delivered a message through Moses which shows the connection between our most mundane family moments and heaven's glorious purposes. It begins with the first and greatest commandment, which was our focus in the early chapters of this book.

> "Listen, Israel: The LORD our God, the LORD is One. Love the LORD your God with all your heart, with all your soul, and with all your strength. These words that I am giving you today are to be in your heart. Repeat them to your children. Talk about them when you sit in your house and when you walk along the road, when you lie down and when you get up. Bind them as a sign on your hand and let them be a symbol on your forehead. Write them on the doorposts of your house and on your gates."

> (Deuteronomy 6:4-9, HCSB)

Notice the sacred importance God has bestowed upon our ordinary moments, "when you sit in your house and when you walk along the road, when you lie down and when you get up." These are the venues where mom and dad pass along their faith to their children.

Please don't miss it: You, mom and dad, are the most powerful influence in the lives of your kids by a long shot. While God has raised up pastors, youth leaders, and Sunday school teachers to serve as wonderful helpers, he never intended for them to replace your role in cultivating an authentic faith in the hearts of your kids. You provide something for your children no one else can: Your day-to-day routine serves as a continual, living and breathing reminder that genuine love for God impacts everything we do. Faith in the Lord is not relegated to an hour on Sunday morning. It's a way of life, a dynamic relationship with the living God.

Where it All Begins

The first step in nurturing a vibrant faith in our kids is to nurture a vibrant faith in ourselves. "These words that I am giving you today," says the Lord, "are to be in your heart." (v.6) Mom and dad, that's where it must begin, making sure the Lord and his word have found a loving home in your heart. We can only pass along to others what is real in our own lives. Our faith will never be perfect, but it must be *authentic*. Our kids must sense intuitively that mom and dad are trying their very best to walk faithfully with the Lord.

Remember, good leadership begins with setting the example for others to follow. Consider what Peter wrote to his church elders and pastors: "Shepherd God's flock among you ... not lording it over those entrusted to you, ***but being examples to the flock.***" (1 Peter 5:2-3, HCSB) Peter cautions his fellow pastors against lording their authority over their congregation, that is, ruling them with a heavy hand. Instead, they were to lead primarily by example. Likewise, we as parents must avoid pounding our faith into our children. That leads to resentment. Passing along the torch of faith begins with our example. It doesn't stop there, but it must begin there.

At this point, if you're feeling inadequate for the job, allow me to congratulate you. You're in a good place. You're coming to terms with the awesome responsibility God has given you. It's a powerful motivation to pray. And pray we should. And rest assured, when our passion lines up with God's passion, amazing things happen through prayer. "The eyes of the LORD search the whole earth in order to strengthen those whose hearts are fully committed to him." (2 Chronicles 16:9, NLT)

All the World a Stage

As soon as you have committed to an authentic walk with the Lord, every nook and corner of family life suddenly shines with glory-potential. As the Lord has said, you'll find endless opportunities to impart your faith to your kids "when you sit in your house and when you walk along the road, when you lie down and when you get up." The routine stuff of life becomes the arena where you show your children "this is what a godly man looks like" or "this is what a godly woman looks like."

At the dinner table, let the kids see mom and dad lead the family in saying thanks for the meal. And pray because you know it's important: God deserves our praise. Let them see dad treat mom with courtesy and hear him thank her for a great meal. Moms, let the kids hear your gentle and respectful words toward dad and see the glad spirit in your service to the family.

Consider what your kids are absorbing at every family meal. Dad, your example conveys to your boys, "This is how a Christian man is supposed to treat his wife." And your daughters are learning, "This is the kind of man I should marry, someone who is loving and kind to his bride." Likewise, mom, your example conveys to your girls the noble image of a godly wife, a loving mom, and a devoted homemaker. And your sons are seeing the qualities they should look for in a wife one day.

When playing backyard football with the kids, dad demonstrates what it looks like to be a good sport both in losing and in winning. When he's trying to sell that clunker of a car in the driveway, he demonstrates his marketplace integrity. When the kids see the kinds of TV shows mom and dad watch, they learn the value of guarding their minds against the corrupt influences in the media. And dad is mindful of maintaining a good attitude toward his job. The kids see him getting up early to get to the office on time.

Are you beginning to see the glory-potential in all those ordinary moments? This truth has been revolutionary for me, I must admit. I'm learning to see amazing opportunity in the most mundane responsibilities of home life. Even those irritating household repairs have become a chance to showcase godly maturity.

True confession: Before our kids came along, household repairs really got under my skin, so much so, I was prone to private temper tantrums when things didn't go right. In my lowest moments, when no one was around to see me, I even threw tools in exasperation. In time, the Lord got my attention and reminded me I had to deal with the roiling impatience in my heart. As James has written, "Human anger does not produce the righteousness God desires." (James 1:20, NLT) God in his mercy brought people into my life who served as winsome examples for me to follow. I watched these servants tackle tough jobs while keeping their composure, even when things went wrong. With a sense of humor, they learned from their mistakes, rolled up their sleeves, and got back to work. That impressed me and encouraged me to build that kind of patience in my own heart.

I'm happy to report I've made a lot of progress. More often than not, I now keep my cool when repairing a leaky faucet, shoveling snow, or painting the lamppost out front. I'm especially happy because I know I've given my boys a much-improved model of how good Christian character keeps its poise even when beset by all those irritants life throws at you.

Let's never forget: Kids are sponges. They soak up our attitudes, our ways of thinking, and how we act in all sorts of circumstances. How many times as an adult did you suddenly realize you were behaving in a manner you had unconsciously picked up from your mom or dad? ("Holy mackerel, *that's* why I scream at other drivers in heavy traffic. That's exactly what my dad did!") That's the power of a parent's example. While all of us are sure to impart some of our quirky mannerisms, bad habits, and unfortunate attitudes, the good news is this: The more we grow toward Christlike maturity, the more good stuff we give our kids to soak up, and they don't even realize it's happening. Think of it as stealth teaching.

Teaching without Preaching

So, encouraging our kids to walk with God begins by setting an example for them to follow, but the Lord also calls us to *talk* to our kids about our faith as well. "These words that I am giving you today are to be in your heart," says the Lord. "Repeat them to your children. Talk about them when you sit in your house and when you walk along the road, when you lie down and when you get up." Notice, God envisions that our relationship with him is such a natural part of our lives, our faith overflows into our daily conversations.

A lot of us parents weren't raised in a home where mom and dad were comfortable talking about God. As soon as someone brought up God-talk, everyone suddenly felt on edge. But that's not what God intended. He wants mom and dad to cultivate an atmosphere where talking about God is the most natural thing in the world and can happen at any moment of the day. If Deuteronomy had been written in our century, it might read something like this: "Talk about the Lord and his word around the breakfast table, when riding to soccer in the mini-van, when sprawled on the family room floor, and when putting on your pajamas at the end of the day."

Once again, God has invested all our moments with amazing glory-potential.

As I reflect on this remarkable passage and consider how to apply it in my own life, I'm aware of a potential hazard: Family life could become very preachy if we aren't careful, where our kids must endure daily sermons from mom and dad. How do we prevent our homes from becoming around-the-clock seminaries? Here are a few suggestions from my own modest wisdom and experience.

First, don't use God, Jesus, the Bible, or the Devil to induce spiritual guilt-trips in your kids. For example, don't be the mom who screams, "What would Jesus say if he saw you pouting like that?!" If a child continually hears that kind of thing, he begins to view God as a tool for manipulating others. Speaking personally, when our kids get in trouble for bad behavior, it's not because they broke God's rules. They know they're in trouble because they broke *dad's* rules. I don't pull out the big King James when disciplining my kids.

I find precedent for this in the book of Proverbs, where we see a father urging his family to follow the path of righteousness: "Listen, my sons ... for I am giving you good instruction. Don't abandon my teaching." (Proverbs 4:1-2, HCSB) Notice the father's plea, "Don't abandon *my* teaching." He's urging his sons to follow *dad's rules.* In time, the kids learn that *God's teaching* has thoroughly shaped *dad's teaching.* I find this approach helps me avoid the hazard of using God as "the bad cop" in the family. There are better times to have the God-centered conversations. And that brings us to the second rule of thumb.

Save the very God-centered conversations for times when everyone is receptive. Remember, a good message delivered at the wrong time can cause more harm than good. As the book of Proverbs reminds us, "If one blesses his neighbor with a loud voice early in the morning, it will be counted as a curse to him." (27:14, IICSB) A blessing is a good thing, but a *loud* blessing *early in the morning* creates resentment. It's a humorous yet insightful reminder to look for the optimal moments to have our God-talks.

It comes down to this: I want my kids to learn that an authentic relationship with the living God is an awesome opportunity, a source of profound fulfillment. "Take delight in the LORD," wrote King David, "and He will give you your heart's desires." (Psalm 37:4, HCSB) I want my kids to see that dad doesn't just obey the Lord, he loves the Lord. Dad *enjoys* the Lord. That's why I look for opportune moments to have those important God-talks when everyone is receptive. It might happen during an informal discussion at the dinner table, or when we're enjoying God's creation on a beautiful spring day, or when we've read a Bible story at bedtime and Levi wants to know why David killed Goliath. I want those talks to be good memories.

Here's a peek into our own family and how I try to follow these principles. Our oldest son Levi, who's five years old at the moment, enjoys playing board games and card games with mom and dad. Early on, we let him win every game. But as he got older, we knew it was important for him to learn how to be a good sport, so mom and dad went for the win at times. At first, this didn't go over well. Levi would throw a fit and sometimes shed tears. On occasion, he resorted to a little creative cheating.

In response, we reminded him how important it is to be a good sport, even when you lose. When his tantrums got really bad or I caught him cheating, I'd get eyeball to eyeball with Levi and say firmly, "Levi, no one likes to play with a cheater. If this is how you're going to act, I'm putting away the game." Sometimes that did the trick. Other times I had to make good on the threat and put the kibosh on our family game time for a while. During those tough talks, Levi sees very clearly how important good sportsmanship is to dad, even catching a wee bit of dad's righteous indignation.

Only later, after the tough talks and tears are over, do I look for opportunities to explain why sportsmanship is so important to me. It all boils down to what God has said, "Treat others the way you want to be treated." I might have that talk later in the day when both of us are calm, when he's ready to listen and I'm able to bring an affectionate spirit to the conversation. Or the talk might happen at bedtime after reading a Bible story. More often than not, those prove to be meaningful conversations for both of us.

On a related note, parents sometimes get uptight because they haven't found the right formula for having family devotions. They try reading Bible stories with the whole family, but the kids are too squirmy. They try devotional books before bed, but everyone's dozing off. So they try having devotions first thing the morning, but that doesn't work either. Soon mom and dad are pushing the panic button. *What's wrong with my family!?*

If you found a formula for consistent family devotions, congratulations! But if you haven't, don't let it get you down. I hope you're beginning to see that God has granted you the whole day to find those teachable moments. Maybe your kids aren't the bookish type who can sit still for a long Bible story. Have those talks at other times. Look for the teachable moments. And remember this: Jesus was the greatest teacher of them all, and some of his most powerful teaching happened outside the classroom.

Third, talk WITH your child, not AT your child. I've noticed an unfortunate tendency among some parents. When they talk to their kids about the Lord, they suddenly feel the need to climb onto a soapbox and begin to lecture. Good ol' dad transforms into a fire and brimstone preacher. He's gone from talking *with* his child to talking *at* his child.

Talking *with* our child requires doing a lot of listening (James 1:19). It means talking on his level as his helper, not talking down to him as his judge. It means, at times, giving him room to make mistakes and figure things out for himself. It means being honest but also being courteous. It means having a soft heart. It means respecting honest questions.

In short, when the God-talks arise, don't bring out the soapbox or that pulpit stored in the hall closet. Your child doesn't need a preacher in those moments. He needs plain ol' mom and dad who are fellow travelers on the road to knowing God better. He needs a mom and dad who are gentle and understanding because, guess what, mom and dad make mistakes too. Our imperfections should remind us to remain humble and gentle in all our relationships, including our relationship with our kids (Hebrews 5:2).

Finally, we come to the fourth and final bit of advice which, I pray, will save us from turning our homes into seminaries: **Love your child as your Heavenly Father loves you.** This is a big one. Christian apologist Josh McDowell coined this bit of wisdom: "Rules without relationship lead to rebellion." What a powerful reminder of why it's important to cultivate a heart-to-heart relationship with our kids. Kids don't want to be mom and dad's spiritual project. They want to be loved and cherished. And the perfect model to follow is our Heavenly Father.

Recall what we learned in the earlier chapters of our journey together: Our Heavenly Father delights in his children. He enjoys being *with* us. He enjoys dining with us. He is not distant; he is personal. He is not cool toward us; he is affectionate. He is not demanding; he is patient. He is not harsh; he is gentle. He went to a lot of trouble so we could enjoy a close, personal relationship with him forever. We are much, much more to him than a spiritual project. We are his very own children, dearly loved, a people close to his heart.

Chapter 17

To the Wife and Mom:
The Glory of Managing a Home

If you're still digging through those seven loads of laundry in search of God's glory, chances are you're a mom at home busy raising the kids and managing the household. All those around-the-clock demands keep the typical mom so busy, she struggles most days to see the nobility of her calling. Moreover, she must contend with the modern sophisticates who persistently deride her chosen vocation, suggesting she's settled in life. It's especially hard to take when someone asks her, "Do you work or are you *just* a homemaker?"

Imagine the audacity of asking someone, "So, you're *just* a contractor?" Or "You're *just* a bookkeeper?" No wonder so many moms at home feel demoralized. When they read their Bibles and see God calling most women to pursue marriage, motherhood, and homemaking, they wonder if God has relegated them to a second-class role.

So, mom, are you struggling to see the glory in raising kids, in loving your husband, in cooking and cleaning and laundry? If so, I believe this chapter will put a smile on your face. I pray God will speak encouragement to you and lead you to embrace your role as a homemaker with a new kind of pride—the good kind of pride that comes from applying yourself to a noble calling.

Walking on Egg Shells

In case you haven't noticed, we are treading on a very sensitive topic, namely, a woman's decision to be a stay-at-home mom or to have a job outside the home. Because it's a deeply personal decision which elicits strong emotions, I want to approach the matter with the right spirit. Careless words could derail this chapter before it ever leaves the station.

In short, here is my opinion: Each family should prayerfully seek God's will and choose what they believe is the best and wisest course. Period. Then, with charity, give other families the freedom to do the same. In the spirit of Romans 14, where Paul shows us how to handle delicate issues, each family should be at peace with their decision without looking down on those who decide differently.

I know it's a little surprising, but in the kingdom of God, two families can reach opposite conclusions on a difficult matter and still be equally approved by the Lord. (See Romans 14:5-7.) Let's face it: No single formula is right for everyone. Each family is different. Each family faces unique challenges. Each season of life requires new strategies. Each woman has her own God-given abilities and aspirations. In the end, what's most important is that we seek God's wisdom and God's will in all matters. May you experience his peace in whatever path you've chosen.

That said, you will discover I wrote much of this chapter with the stay-at-home mom in mind, especially the mom raising small children. Because this messed-up world tends to elevate job-success over home-success, the stay-at-home mom is especially prone to feeling demoralized in her work. For that reason, I'm giving her special attention.

Really, this chapter is dedicated to all the homemakers out there: to the moms with full-time jobs, part-time jobs, or no jobs outside the home, to the married moms and the single moms. Whoever you are, whatever road you're traveling, this chapter is for you. And as we've seen time and again, God's grand purpose for each of us transcends our circumstances. There is more glory than you ever thought possible right in your own home.

One of the Hardest Jobs in the World

Moms, let's begin by giving credit where credit is due. Your job is incredibly demanding, arguably one of the most difficult jobs on earth. I have talked to women from all sorts of backgrounds, and I hear the same refrain: Raising small children at home was the most challenging and most stressful job they ever had. Many of these same women have proven themselves bright and capable in the job world, but the challenge of being a stay-at-home mom pushed them to the edge.

A few years ago, I was reading *American Sniper,* the autobiography of Chris Kyle, a decorated Navy SEAL who served four tours in Iraq. When he came home from deployment, he had to face the stress of being around a crying baby. His wife Taya, who adds her perspective throughout the book, wrote this: "Chris had trouble handling the baby's crying at first, and that stressed me as well—you can handle war but you can't handle a few days of crying...?"

A lot of us men would agree: Handling the stress of war is preferable, some days, to handling the stress of a crying baby. So, moms, when it comes to managing the kids, even Navy SEALs, among the toughest men in the military, admire your grit. It takes a special talent from the Lord to show love and tenderness day after day to that fussy, demanding but oh-so-precious lump of infant humanity.

Despite your giftedness, however, you are only human and prone to the effects of stress. It's the nature of the work. And when you're in the valley—fatigued, frustrated, and overwhelmed—you're tempted to question your mom-credentials. Your days often feel terribly unproductive and downright futile. One mom, whose kids are now in their teens, expressed to me the deep frustration that came with raising small children: "I cannot begin to express how profoundly unproductive I felt every day." I now understand what she meant. I can't even count the number of times Megan has ended the day in a pall of defeat. "I got absolutely nothing done today!"

I can only sympathize. When I was home alone with our three boys during their high maintenance years, trying to complete the simplest project becomes a Herculean task because of all the interruptions: *Someone's stinky. Who needs a diaper change? ... Oops, it's snack time already ... Why is Lucas crying? Oh, he can't find his blanky ... Why is it so quiet? They must be getting into something. Better go check ... NOW who's stinky? Time for another diaper change ... Now Marcus is asking for his water sippy. I just gave him a water sippy. Where is it? Darn it, I can't find it. I'll just fill up another one. Here ... What was that crash? Of course, Lucas just pulled the highchair over on himself. Now he's trapped and crying. That's going to leave a mark ... Finally, a moment's peace...What's that smell? NOW who's stinky...?*

In dealing with the futility, I've traversed all five steps of coping: denial, frustration, anger, resignation, and finally acceptance. I just assumed I would get nothing else done when home alone with the kids. That way I'm less inclined to get frustrated. My motto became, "It's always *something*." So, moms, I understand why some days you feel exasperated for having gotten nothing done all day. The truth is, you got lots of things done. It's just that you have an army of mini-humans undoing faster than you can do.

Oh, and did I mention you're always on call, that you get no days off, nights off, or accrued vacation? Your work schedule recognizes none of the major holidays. And when you're sick, everyone still expects you to do your job. Yeah, I know it's not fair. When dad's sick, he stays home from work, sleeps all day, and expects you to measure out his Nyquil.

Again, a word of encouragement to mom: You're not crazy. Being a mom, especially of young kids, really is one of the hardest jobs in the world. May God bless you every day. I for one could never do what you do. I think most men, the honest ones anyway, would agree one hundred and fifty percent.

Yes, it's a Real Job!

Now that we've established being a homemaker is one of the toughest jobs in the world, I hope you can view yourself as having a bona fide and respectable vocation. Never think of yourself as *just* a homemaker.

Don't be intimidated by the job-snobs in the world, those who believe success comes only from a career that pays you money. These sophisticates roll their eyes with disdain at the mom who can whip up a delicious dinner for her family, but they heap praises on the woman who gets paid as a chef to prepare meals for strangers. They sigh with boredom when women choose to stay home to raise the kids, but they shower accolades on the woman who opens a daycare center to raise other people's kids. Do you see the irony?

Just so I'm not misunderstood, I'm not suggesting all women should be stay-at-home moms. Not at all. I'm simply shining a light on the twisted value system that underlies people's thinking, the idea that receiving money in return for work somehow makes the work more admirable and the woman more of a success story.

Is that how God measures someone's importance, in terms of dollars and cents? Of course not. When a woman chooses to do what's best for her family *out of genuine love for them*, that's what earns God's heartfelt approval, whether that means staying home or getting an outside job. Remember, love is the highest virtue in God's kingdom, not your earning power. I'm confident that Jesus, who was rich but for our sakes become poor, would agree (2 Corinthians 8:9).

Your New Title: Home Manager

Okay, mom, it's time to bestow on you a title worthy of your vocation. You are no longer a homemaker; you are now a home manager. This title is rooted in how God views your work. The apostle Paul employed this term when he counseled the young widows in Ephesus "...to marry, have children, [and] manage their households." (1 Timothy 5:14, HCSB) The Greek verb for "managing the household" is a potent term. Some translations render it as *ruling* the household (RSV, ASV). Here's the point: *Managing* a home is not a tepid concept. It describes someone who is enterprising and skillful in handling her responsibilities.

So, congratulations! You've just been promoted to management. I wish I could offer a raise to go with the promotion, but the truth is, no one could afford to pay you all that overtime.

Some might wonder how a mom can be a strong, take-charge home manager when God has appointed the husband as the head of the home (Ephesians 5:23). Really, there is no contradiction. We see this kind of arrangement in the job world all the time. Consider a businessman who owns a thriving manufacturing company. While he is the head of the business, he employs an army of capable people working under him, all of them experts in own their field, whether its finance, sales, engineering, or technical support. Most of these specialists know far more about their area of expertise than the boss does. And that's okay. The boss is glad to have such a capable team. He values the skillful expert who can make the business more effective.

In the same way, God never intended for the husband's headship to squash the wife's enterprising spirit. If that's what's happening, someone in the marriage has a distorted view of leadership. God has not given the man authority to lord it over his family. (See Mark 10:42-44.) Rather, leadership is a position of service, and the godly husband uses his influence to encourage his wife and kids to bloom to their fullest potential. The wise husband is grateful to God when his wife shows amazing ingenuity in juggling all the details involved in managing a home.

We'll talk more about the man's leadership in the next chapter. For now, it's enough for us to understand that the husband's leadership and the wife's enterprising spirit are designed to meld together like a hand and glove. They are not competitors but team players, each thriving in their God-given role. In fact, the Lord provides an inspiring portrait of just such an enterprising home manager in Proverbs 31, what has been called an ode to the noble wife.

Uh, oh. At this point, some women in my reading audience are groaning in the spirit because they have a phobic aversion to Proverbs 31. They're weary of being compared to the perfect mom. Don't worry. You'll find no discouraging comparisons here. Instead, I want to help you see how Proverbs 31 is full of affirmation for you. You have more in common with the noble wife than you realize. Prepare to be inspired.

Martha Stewart Meets Mother Teresa?

Scripture's ode to the noble wife in Proverbs 31 is either famous or infamous, depending on who you talk to. The wife described in poetic verse is a paragon of talent and virtue, so I understand why some women approach the chapter with dismay. It's easy to develop an inferiority complex when comparing yourself to the embodiment of Martha Stewart and Mother Teresa; so, if you're a little intimidated, here are a few words of encouragement to keep things in proper perspective.

First, be careful you don't reduce Proverbs 31 to a mere list of things to do. (If you are a wife and mom, chances are your to-do list is already way too long.) Instead, I want you to view the passage as an expression of what God values, a clue to what pleases the heart of your Heavenly Father. With that simple change of perspective, something amazing happens. Suddenly, you discover that your work as a home manager is near and dear to God's heart, that there is incredible glory in the ordinary, even in those seven piles of laundry.

Second, if the noble wife in Proverbs 31 fills you with apprehension, I urge you to keep something in mind. All of us, men and women alike, measure ourselves against an impossible standard every day—the holy and loving character of Jesus Christ. Still, we love him and aspire to be like him. God already knows our shortcomings, and he loves us anyway. He never condemns us; rather he is fully committed to us. We are free to follow him with hearts full of hope, knowing we have a promising future, regardless of the failures in our past.

So, if this chapter begins to overwhelm you rather than inspire you, why not return to the early chapters for a little while and review all the mercies God has shown us despite our flaws? (See chapters four and five in the section "His Heart Beats for You.") Read, reflect, and embrace these beautiful truths until you're awash in the peace of Jesus Christ. Really, there's no reason to feel dismayed by the noble wife. Don't view her as a measuring stick. View her as a hero. Heroes earn our admiration, and they stoke the fires in our hearts.

Oh, here's one more antidote for fighting the guilts. Most commentators agree that the noble wife described in Proverbs 31 is not an actual person. She's an ideal, the poetic expression of the highest virtues of being a wife, mother, and home manager. That's why we see only her good days in the passage and none of her bad days. Trust me. All real human beings have bad days. Now then, let's turn to Proverbs 31 and pop open this three-thousand-year-old can of inspiration.

Priceless

If you want to know what's truly important in life, look to the Lord for the answer because his verdict is all that matters. For that reason alone, Proverbs 31 contains a wealth of encouragement to all the dedicated home managers out there because, as you will soon discover, he cherishes all you do as a wife and mom. Clearly, you have his attention. The ode to the noble wife opens this way:

> Who can find a capable wife?
> She is far more precious than jewels.
> The heart of her husband trusts in her,
>   and he will not lack anything good.
> She rewards him with good, not evil,
>   all the days of her life.

(Proverbs 31:10-12, HCSB)

The poem begins, "Who can find a capable wife?" Don't let the question throw you. The poet is not despairing that there aren't any virtuous wives around. He's simply employing rhetorical flourish to express what an invaluable blessing she is to the man who finds her. In fact, he goes on to write, "She is far more precious than jewels."

Please don't miss it. The woman who pours her life into her family is a treasure, both to the Lord and to her family. And it remains true even when your husband and children take you for granted, which tends to happen a lot. We don't sing your praises enough, so please take this opportunity to be refreshed in your spirit. Let the Lord brag on you for a little while.

His praise continues: "The heart of her husband trusts in her, and he will not lack anything good. She rewards him with good, not evil, all the days of her life." (vv.11-12) Rest assured, ladies, you are a wealth of goodness to your husband. God is the one who fashioned you to be the perfect companion for him (Genesis 2:18). God endowed you with beauty, charm, softness, and a way of feeling and thinking which bring completion to his life, and this remains true despite all your imperfections. God, the master craftsman, made you to be a blessing!

Skillful Hands

As the poem unfolds, the Lord draws attention to the specialized skill set of this noble wife. Because she hails from a culture quite different from our own, her daily tasks may strike you as unfamiliar. Once you peel back the cultural trappings, however, you'll discover how much you have in common. See if you can spot the similarities between a home manager today and a home manager in ancient Israel.

> She selects wool and flax
>   and works with willing hands.
> She is like the merchant ships,
>   bringing her food from far away.
> She rises while it is still night
>   and provides food for her household
>   and portions for her female servants.

(Proverbs 31:13-15, HCSB)

"She selects wool and flax." (v.13) In other words, she's gathering supplies to keep her family clothed. Flax, by the way, is a fibrous plant used to make linen.

At this point, a lot of women feel threatened by the noble wife because "Oh, my gosh! She's making her own clothes! I have no idea how to make my own clothes!" Rest assured, God is not commanding you to become an expert seamstress. That's not the point. The point is, the noble wife works hard to keep her family clothed, just like you do.

The noble wife lived in an era when the economics of the day required a lot of households to fashion their own wardrobes from scratch. When dad needed a new tunic, mom didn't dash to Walmart and browse the men's section. Instead, if she didn't have cloth on hand, she selected the raw wool or flax to make thread. Then she used a loom to weave the thread into fabric. We see her doing just that in v.19: "She extends her hands to the spinning staff, and her hands hold the spindle."

Today, even among the most accomplished seamstresses, it's rare to find one who spins her own thread! So, don't let the difference in cultures distract you. Here's the thing to notice: The wife's day-in and day-out work to supply the family's wardrobe has earned God's applause, whether the woman fashions clothes from scratch, buys them at Walmart, or finds them in a thrift store. As mundane as these domestic chores might seem, God deems them worthy of his praise.

The poem continues: "She is like the merchant ships, bringing her food from far away." (v.14) Here we find the noble wife grocery shopping. Of course, the poet elevates her work by comparing her to a merchant ship which, time and again, delivers delicacies to the family table. "Food from far away" suggests she visits the exotic food aisle from time to time and serves up something Chinese or Mexican. Again, the Lord is showing us the glory in our ordinary. What we view as a mundane chore—going for groceries of all things—God elevates as laudable and exemplary.

"She rises while it is still night," writes the poet, "and provides food for her household and portions for her female servants." (v.15)

Here's a timeless scene as true now as it was then: Mom gets up early, while it's still dark outside, to pack everyone's lunch. The work of a home manager requires early mornings and late nights. Even while the rest of the family remains snuggled in bed, mom is in the kitchen before sunup assembling baloney sandwiches. And God knows because he's right there with her, praising her hard work.

Consider what we've learned so far. The Lord, speaking through the poet who wrote Proverbs 31, has waxed eloquent about the diligence and the domestic skills of the noble wife. She is worthy of our highest admiration. Why then do so many moms struggle to view their home management profession as praiseworthy? And, yes, being a home manager is a *profession*.

Professionalism is about pride, skill, and integrity as much as it is about being paid. We've all met paid professionals who do business in a terribly unprofessional way. It's the attitude, not the paycheck that counts. So, mom, it's okay to look in the mirror from time to time and take pride in your professional acumen. Consider how much you have grown in all your skills since the day you were married. Imagine having to hire a "replacement mom" for your household. How much training would she require, assuming she sticks around after discovering all the unpaid overtime the position demands?

Consider all the vocational skills of the typical home manager: She's a child psychologist. (A mom is great at reading her kids whether she has the clinical degree or not. It comes from intuition plus experience.) She's skilled in child development, logistics, time management, the culinary arts, basic medical diagnosis, finances, purchasing, bargain hunting, inventory management, and supply acquisition. Really, the home manager runs a not-for-pay child care center, full-time bed and breakfast (plus lunch and dinner), hospitality center, social hall, and infirmary.

Are you beginning to see why the diligent home manager has inspired the poet to sing her praises? Her ministry to her family requires an incredible breadth of skill and heartfelt devotion.

Strong and Enterprising

There's something else I want you to see in Proverbs 31: The noble wife exemplifies how a woman is free to bring all her talents, her personal flair, as well as an enterprising spirit to her work.

> She evaluates a field and buys it;
>> she plants a vineyard with her earnings.
> She draws on her strength
>> and reveals that her arms are strong.
> She sees that her profits are good,
>> and her lamp never goes out at night.

(Proverbs 31:16–18, HCSB)

We get the distinct impression this noble wife has some business acumen, the way she buys, sells, and trades in the marketplace. At this point, some of you might find her capabilities a bit intimidating. If so, you're not alone. I'm feeling a little intimidated myself. As a man, it's not easy to meet a woman who has more business moxie than I do.

However, there's no need for any of us to be intimidated. We can rest happily in the promise that God created each one of us with unique gifts and abilities, all tailor-made to fulfill our God-given purpose in his kingdom. Yes, the noble wife can clear a cool profit at the village bazaar like it's nobody's business, but that's because God created her to do just that. Yes, she has a God-given gift, but so do you.

Don't get hung up on the fact that you don't have the same gifts you see in someone else. We're *supposed* to be different. As a community of believers, our differences are designed to make us greater than the sum of our parts. (See 1 Corinthians 12:12-27.) God made each of us unique on purpose and *for* a purpose. He endowed you with a personalized gift-set in keeping with the unique plan he has for you. You are now free to admire the noble wife (or any other woman for that matter) and say, "You go, girl!" while rejoicing in your own special work God has given you to do.

The bottom line is this: Sometimes home managers feel confined in their role because they've bought into a narrow template of what a proper wife and mom ought to be. They feel squeezed into a mold that just doesn't fit their God-given style. The enterprising spirit of the noble wife, however, should inspire any home manager to bring her own personal flair to the role.

Really, when a woman invests her God-given talents into home and family, all sorts of dividends are possible. For some, it means pulling in extra spending money for the family. For the woman who's an artist at heart, she'll beautify the home with splashes of creativity. Another woman with a knack for hospitality transforms the house into the go-to place for the kids in the neighborhood or a fellowship center for the church. A woman with administrative acumen keeps the checkbook balanced and the husband and the kids all running on time. The possibilities are limited only by the woman's imagination.

Behind Every Great Man

When we leap ahead in this passage, we find some biographical information about the man of the family. "...Her husband is known at the city gates, where he sits among the elders of the land." (31:23) The city gates, in those days, served as the civic center where official town business was conducted. Thus, we discover her husband is a man of some importance, highly respected among his peers.

Wait a minute! This poem is about the wife. Why is the man trying to steal the spotlight? To illustrate a universal truth which, even today, remains preserved in proverbial form: Behind every great man stands a great woman. The noble wife is indispensable to her husband's success. Why should we be surprised at this? God created woman to be the perfect counterpart for her husband (Genesis 2:18).

This hints at a profound truth. We know from Scripture that God intended for marriage to model the relationship between Christ and his people. (See Ephesians 5:22–24.) The husband, when he is at his best, serves as a picture of Jesus' love and headship. The wife, when she is at her best, serves as a picture of how the church brings glory to Christ. In fact, Paul writes, "Woman is man's glory." (1 Corinthians 11:7, HCSB) Think about it: The church glorifies Christ by making his greatness visible to the world; the wife glorifies her husband in a similar way, by bringing out his greatness in the world. She causes him to shine, you might say.

For those who have fallen under the spell of radical feminism, this truth is deeply offensive because the wife, it seems, plays second fiddle to the man. But, once again, such thinking has bought into the world's shallow value system. The glory of being a woman comes into sharp focus when we choose to see things from God's perspective, and God makes it very clear that the wife, because of her influence in the family, shares in her husband's success. No wonder Proverbs 31 showers her with accolades.

> Her sons rise up and call her blessed.
> Her husband also praises her:
> "Many women are capable,
>   but you surpass them all!"

...Give her the reward of her labor,
and let her works praise her at the city gates.

(Proverbs 31:28–31, HCSB)

In those final lines, "...let her works praise her at the city gates," I sense the Holy Spirit has a message for the dedicated home manager: *God has noticed all your devotion and hard work. Remain faithful, for you will receive a rich reward. You will enter the gates of eternal glory in triumph, to the roar of thunderous applause.*

Final Thoughts for the Journey

As I bring this chapter to a close, I want to return to the idea that a godly wife and mother has a glorifying influence on her family. Her loving devotion, however imperfect, encourages her family to bloom in ways that offer the world a stirring picture of God's goodness. And, oh, how we need that influence today.

The "enlightened" ones have insisted for decades that marriage is inherently oppressive and that raising children is beneath any self-respecting woman. Our hearts are broken as we witness the terrible consequences of our nation's decision to abandon God's wonderful plan for the family, the very fabric of society.

But the pseudointellectual arguments for the secular lifestyle don't hold up very well when held next to a real-life family where God's love and wisdom are evident. Suddenly, those vogue theories appear shallow and selfish in comparison. We see the nobility of Christlike leadership in the Christian husband. We see the tender and sacrificial love of God in the Christian mom. We see God's wisdom vindicated as his teaching bears fruit in the lives of their children.

Here's the point: Moms, your selfless ministry to your family brings much-needed light to a dark world. Don't let the critics discourage you. You are a blessing in ways you don't even realize.

Years ago, I knew a young lady who admitted she was eager to get married and raise a family. Why? Because, as a woman, she could think of no higher privilege than to raise a godly man and send him out into the world. Wow, what an amazing reminder that God has invited the wife and mother toward an honorable vocation, one of powerful influence for good.

Perhaps, mom, you need that reminder today. It's easy to lose sight of the glory while enduring those tough days of family life, where the job seems impossible and you feel inadequate to the task. Remember, God is with you in this. Today's storm will pass as it always does. Smoother waters are ahead. That's the nature of family. We'll experience smooth and blessed seas at times, but the next storm is always on the horizon. But stay on course! A land of eternal rewards awaits at the end of your journey.

Recently I was passing through our kitchen when I overheard Megan and the boys playing a boardgame together in the family room. They were laughing and having a great time together. In that moment, I caught a glimpse of all the wonderful blessings Megan brings to our family, even though she has a hard time seeing it most days. In the years ahead, as our boys become men and enter the world, they will reap goodness for the rest of their lives, all because they had a mom who loved God and selflessly loved her family. And I haven't even mentioned all the blessings Megan brings to me. That would require writing another book.

Moms, I pray God will open your eyes to the blessings you bring to your family, and I pray he'll renew your spirit so you don't grow weary in doing good. You will reap a rich reward if you don't give up (Galatians 6:9).

When you enter eternal glory one day, accolades will greet you at the city gate, and you will hear your husband and children among the voices saying, "We all rise up and call you blessed. You have worked so hard and sacrificed so much on our behalf. You are long overdue for a rich reward."

And finally, mom, you'll have that day off you've been longing for. Yes, there's a long, hard journey between now and then, but it will be so worth it. And on that day, as God invites you to share in his eternal happiness, you will hear him say, "Well done, child. Well done."

Chapter 18

To the Husband and Dad:
The Glory of Leading a Family

Recently, something depressing happened while I waited for the latest *Star Wars* movie to begin at our local cinema. A spellbinding scene suddenly splashed across the movie screen. Animated heroes engaged in glorious battle. The sounds of war filled the theater. A blood-stirring orchestral score thundered in the background. It was inspiring stuff. Finally, the tagline appeared: "Greatness Awaits." Then came the big reveal: It was a promotion for the latest video game console.

Er, what?

Apparently, men can find greatness by pretending to be heroes in the make-believe world of video games. Yeah, I know, I shouldn't have taken the ad so seriously. It's just a marketing gimmick after all, but I'm afraid it reveals more about the current state of manhood than we care to admit.

You see, when men lose sight of their God-given opportunity for greatness, they settle for shallow substitutes. Consider the caricature of manhood pedaled in the typical sitcom: The father is bored with his humdrum suburban existence. Tied down by his family and his job, he regrets giving up the excitement of the single life when he was free to fornicate, pursue his own dreams, and shun responsibility. His wife hovers over him like a mother figure, reining in dad's immature behavior. His sex life is dull if it exists at all. He is a boy in a man's body, never able to figure out how to be the adult.

Ugh, no wonder men struggle to live out their God-given potential, having bought into a juvenile version of masculinity. There is nothing to rouse a man's soul toward greatness. So, where does a man find masculine glory? Is it in his golf score, the size of his business, or in the expensive car he drives? Does greatness come from power and influence, economic status, or social standing? Will he find it in a university degree, by acquiring a trophy wife, or by defeating the boss villain in *Zombie Carnage Apocalypse IV*?

The answer is "none of the above."

In keeping with what we've learned already, a man's pathway to glory passes right through the ordinary stuff of life. Indeed, greatness awaits any man who sets his heart on pursuing Christlike masculinity, and that means becoming the husband and father God calls him to be.

That last paragraph probably irked some people. First, it irked those men who assume Jesus is a Marvin Milquetoast kind of guy, a role model for feminized masculinity. If that's your vision of Jesus, you've been badly misinformed. In just a few short paragraphs, you'll meet the real Jesus, and you'll discover he's the stuff heroes are made of. Seriously, prepare to be inspired.

There's a second group of people who are likely irked by the term Christlike masculinity, namely, the feminists of the radical left. They are hellbent on turning men into women (or women into men, it's all kind of confusing). For decades now, they've preached that gender distinctions are artificial and downright harmful. Despite their best efforts, however, they find themselves thwarted by the instincts God has programmed into the human heart.

When I attended college years ago, radical feminism was already rampant on campus. Tara, one of the young women in my circle of friends, drank deeply of the ideology. She viewed traditional distinctions between men and women as artificial and oppressive. It sparked quite a few lively conversations between us.

One weekend, a group of us attended a movie showing in the student center. The hero on screen was a winsome and rugged man who exhibited the traditional masculine qualities we admire: He was courageous, a skillful hunter and provider, had a clever sense of humor, and he protected the woman in his care. The female lead was a cosmopolitan type from the big city who was turned off by our hero at first. But, as you might expect, she ends up falling in love with him, swept off her feet by his alluring masculinity.

As the final credits rolled, my friend Tara turned and looked at me with dreamy eyes. Clearly, the hero on screen had swept Tara off her feet as well, and I was happy to point out the irony: The guy in the movie represented everything she had argued against in the name of feminism. And yet as soon as she saw a man portrayed as the strong protector and romantic lover, her female heart swooned. She could not escape the magnetic pull of God's design. "Toxic masculinity" turned out to be not-so-toxic after all.

Yes, there is something inspiring about a strong man of character. He still inspires. And women still swoon. *That*, men, is a picture of Jesus Christ.

Jesus the Hero

Men want to be heroes, and women want to be loved by them. It's all part of the male-female dynamic God wove into our being, and that dynamic, which reaches its fullest potential in marriage, serves as a portrait of God's relationship to his people.

When we think of marriage as a divinely-inspired portrait, Ephesians chapter five likely comes to mind, where we learn the husband serves as a picture of Christ while the wife serves as a picture of the church (Ephesians 5:22-33). This beautiful passage, penned by the apostle Paul, is familiar to many of us because it's the go-to Scripture reading in wedding ceremonies and has inspired many sermons from the pulpit.

The Christ-as-husband imagery did not begin with Paul, however. It preceded him by centuries. Throughout the Old Testament, God described his relationship to his people as a marriage. "For your Creator will be your husband," says Isaiah the prophet, "the LORD of Heaven's Armies is his name!" (Isaiah 54:5, NLT) Ezekiel expresses this same truth in a passage that is shocking in its detail:

> [The LORD says to his people Israel:] "And when I passed by again, I saw that you were old enough for love. So I wrapped my cloak around you to cover your nakedness and declared my marriage vows. I made a covenant with you, says the Sovereign LORD, and you became mine.
>
> "...I gave you lovely jewelry, bracelets, beautiful necklaces, a ring for your nose, earrings for your ears, and a lovely crown for your head .... Your clothes were made of fine linen and costly fabric and were beautifully embroidered. You ate the finest foods...and became more beautiful than ever. You looked like a queen, and so you were!"
>
> (Ezekiel 16:8-13, NLT)

Is it any wonder a beautiful wedding ceremony resonates so deeply? It stirs the timeless yearnings God has placed in the hearts of men and women. Men want to be the strong provider who lavishes gifts on his bride. The woman wants to be the queen of the home who is beautiful in the eyes of her husband. It's all God's design, a living metaphor of the love relationship between God and his redeemed.

Not only does the husband, on his best days, reflect the love of Christ, he also reflects the power and the majesty of Christ. We see this clearly in Psalm 45 where Jesus appears as a handsome, conquering king on his wedding day, and his bride swoons over his winsome blend of strength and humility. The bride, of course, represents the church Jesus loves and to whom he is wedded forever. If this interpretation sounds bizarre, rest assured, the New Testament affirms the psalm's Messianic significance. (See Hebrews 1:8-9.) The psalm even discloses Jesus' divinity, centuries before his miracle birth (Psalm 45:6-7). The passage is a stirring, prophetic picture of the sacred romance between Jesus and his people. Read, now, the words of the poet:

> Beautiful words stir my heart.
>   I will recite a lovely poem about the king,
>   for my tongue is like the pen of a skillful poet.
> You [King Jesus the groomsman]
>   are the most handsome of all.
>   Gracious words stream from your lips.
>   God himself has blessed you forever.
> Put on your sword, O mighty warrior!
>   You are so glorious, so majestic!
> In your majesty, ride out to victory,
>   defending truth, humility, and justice.
>   Go forth to perform awe-inspiring deeds!
>
> ...Listen to me, O royal daughter [the bride];
>   take to heart what I say.
>   Forget your people and your family far away.

For your royal husband delights in your beauty;
honor him, for he is your lord.

(Psalm 45:1-4, 10-11, NLT)

This vision of Jesus as the conquering hero looks ahead to his glorious return at the end of the age. (See Revelation 19:11-16.) He is the ideal man, displaying the kind of noble masculinity which inspires us all. He is both gracious and majestic, the warrior who fights, not for himself, but for truth and justice, the one who employs his power to rescue the humble. And he delights in the beauty of his bride who is resplendent on her wedding day.

This arresting image is imprinted on the human heart so deeply, it permeates our literature and movies: The courageous hero rescues the woman in distress. Despite centuries of retelling, the story still resonates when told with skillful artistry. In the movies, when the righteous champion comes to the rescue, women still swoon, and men still point at the screen and say, "I want to be like that guy."

Are you beginning to see that true masculinity is a glorious thing? When God calls you to represent Christ in your marriage, it's an invitation to greatness. In fact, Jesus came to our world, suffered, died, and rose again to bring many sons to glory, the glory we left behind in Eden. (See Hebrews 2:10.) Jesus Christ wants to lead you to become the kind of man, deep down, you always wanted to be. He invites you to become a loving warrior, a hero in the eyes of your family. And he wants your bride to swoon at your greatness.

Act Like Men!

Let's press on and blow the dust off an obscure verse Paul wrote to the men in the church of Corinth. "Be courageous; be strong. Do everything in love." (1 Corinthians 16:13-14, NIV) While this is a fine rendering, let us turn to a translation that is more literal and, as a result, a bit more jarring: "***Act like men***, be strong. Let all that you do be done in love." (NASB)

I must confess, I love Paul's call to arms. *Act like men! Be strong!* He reminds us that strength is masculine. Strength is good. But our strength must always be guided by love. What a beautiful summary of godly masculinity, strength wrapped in love. It's the picture of the loving warrior. As the poet extolled in Psalm 45, "Put on your sword, O mighty warrior! ... Defending truth, humility, and justice." Men are the warriors of society. We are to rise above fear and timidity (2 Timothy 1:7). The righteous are as bold as lions (Proverbs 28:1).

This is a side of Jesus people often overlook. Yes, he was gentle and humble at heart, but he was also strong and courageous. He knew how to exercise boldness when needed. When he saw the moneychangers defiling the temple courts with their greed, he ignited a righteous brawl, overturning tables and driving the merchants away (Matthew 21:12). And if he had something to say, he was the kind of man who looked you in the eye and spoke the truth in perfect wisdom and perfect love (Matthew 16:23).

This is the same Jesus who publicly dressed down the corrupt religious officials of his day: "Woe to you, scribes and Pharisees, hypocrites! You travel over land and sea to make one proselyte, and when he becomes one, you make him twice as fit for hell as you are!" (Matthew 23:15, HCSB) Most men would agree: One of the hardest character-tests we face is having to choose between doing the easy thing which is popular or doing the righteous thing which requires standing alone. Jesus won that battle every time. Jesus was no wilting daisy.

So, men, when we talk about developing Christlike masculinity as a husband and father, we have set our sights on a goal that is profoundly inspiring. God calls us onward and upward toward becoming the strong protectors of our families. We are to exemplify

Christ's lordship as well as his humility, his strength as well as his gentleness, his courage as well as his tenderhearted love.

At this point, I imagine some men are perplexed at this call to courage. "All this sounds way over-the-top," they say. "We're talking about being good husbands and fathers. How hard can it be? Who needs a warrior's heart to do that?" The truth is, any man who wishes to become a godly husband and father will need to cultivate the heart of a warrior. Think of it this way: God has appointed the man to be head of his home. (More on that shortly.) It's a position of leadership. But what are the great temptations men face when it comes to fulfilling their duties to family? Passivity, inaction, indifference—often borne out of fear.

When men shrink from their responsibilities at home, they don't think of it as acting out of fear. They think of it as "just doing guy-stuff." They escape to their man cave. Or they immerse themselves in the internet or video games. They put in tons of overtime at work. Or they bury themselves in time-consuming hobbies. Or they hang out with the guys at the Lonely Hearts Tavern. Or they abdicate leadership by mumbling to their wives, "Whatever. I don't care. Do what you want."

Guys, let's be honest. The stress of family responsibilities, in the tough times, can push us to the edge, and it takes a warrior's heart to persevere. A lot of men have developed the warrior's heart in their careers, they've developed the warrior's heart on the ballfield, but they have yet to pursue the highest calling of all, to become a warrior for the good of their families.

Consider the typical challenges a dad faces. He arrives home from work, exhausted from a long day, and discovers mom and the kids are in meltdown mode, complete with screaming and crying. It takes moral fortitude to enter the fray and become the calming influence that's needed— while avoiding a meltdown of his own.

When a man realizes his wife is less than inspired by his romantic overtures, that's a real ego-killer. He wants to slink away and stop trying. It takes courage to stay at it, to risk rejection, to admit he has things to learn, to work hard at becoming the kind of lover his wife desires.

When a man's son enters adolescence, dad knows it's time to sit down with him and have "the talk," an honest discussion about the moral temptations men face and how to remain pure in a sex-obsessed world.

When his daughter is old enough to start dating, dad dares to be one of those old-fashioned types who insists on personally meeting any guy who wants to take her out. Their first date will always be at the family dinner table.

When dad is laid off from work and the bills are piling up, he needs to be the pillar of strength the family needs. They need to see dad's quiet confidence in the Lord. They need to hear him say, "Everything's going to be okay."

When everyone else at the office has made work and career their highest priorities in life, it takes real grit for a man to swim against the tide. Yes, his job at the office is important, but it's not the only job he has. God has appointed him as leader and shepherd of his family. That's a trust that must be protected and honored. It requires making tough choices.

A husband walks into the kitchen and discovers his wife is sullen and deathly quiet. *Uh, oh. What's wrong? What have I done now?* A lot of men, in response, will find someplace to hide until the storm passes, hence the invention of the man cave. But the man whose heart is full of love and courage will kindly probe his wife's heart to find out what's wrong. He's willing to endure painful criticism, whether deserved or not, to mend the relationship.

Are you getting the picture? Answering the call to be a godly husband and father is not for the faint of heart.

Okay, before I go much further, it's time for a reality check. I'm painting a rather lofty picture of Christian masculinity. My intent, as I've said all along, is to inspire our hearts, to rekindle our motivation to become loving warriors in the way Christ is. That said, I have a confession to make: In this chapter, I'm writing checks that, some days, my body can't cash. You see, I'm very much a work in progress like you are. But the ideal of Christian masculinity is so compelling, I've decided that's the kind of man I want to be. So, I keep pressing forward. As Paul has written, "Not that I have already obtained this or am already perfect, but I press on to make it my own, because Christ Jesus has made me his own." (Philippians 3:12, ESV)

What about you? Are you feeling inspired or overwhelmed? I have a hunch some of you are overwhelmed. If the seed of a loving warrior ever existed in your heart, you fear it died a long time ago. Maybe it was your upbringing. Maybe you've been brainwashed by the gender-bending ideology of radical feminism. Whatever the reason, you never cultivated the masculine part of your soul.

If that's where you find yourself, I can relate to your struggle, completely! For most of my life, I was stuck in that very spot. But God showed me a way out, and I want to share my story for your encouragement. It's not enough for you to see the glory of Christlike masculinity. I want you to believe beyond all doubt that God can take you there.

Finding Your Inner Warrior

I'm still embarrassed to admit it, but when Megan and I got married, I was ill-suited to be the strong and loving leader of our home. Part of the struggle came from my natural temperament which tended toward timidity. And all through my youth, I avoided scary challenges rather than accept them as growth opportunities. So, for most of my life, fear dominated my emotions, and the masculine part of my soul withered from neglect.

When I finally embarked on that grand adventure called marriage, all those unresolved insecurities haunted me with a vengeance. I was not the strong and steady partner Megan thought she had married. Marriage was my wakeup call. I had a lot of growing up to do in a short time. It was a long process and painful for both of us, but God has shown me how to develop the heart of a righteous warrior.

Here's what I learned, and here's what I want to pass along to you: We can *condition* ourselves toward strength and courage. "Train yourself in godliness," writes Paul (1 Timothy 4:7, HCSB). Like any muscle in the body, your courage muscles will grow stronger the more you flex them. Remember, God told Joshua, "Be strong and courageous." (Joshua 1:6) Notice, it's a command. That means there's an element of strength and courage that is a *choice*. We can develop the virtues of Godly masculinity by daily *choosing* the pathways that require strength and courage, and that's the direction the Spirit of God wants to lead us. "For God has not given us a spirit of fearfulness, but one of power, love, and sound judgment." (2 Timothy 1:7, HCSB)

Not long ago, I was gobbling up books and movies on the real-life exploits of our military's elite forces. I immersed myself in the world of the Navy SEALS, the Army Rangers, and the Army's secretive Delta Force. What amazed me was the grueling intensity of their training, designed to push each man to the breaking point. And those who graduated learned they were capable of tackling challenges that once seemed impossible. They attained a level of strength and courage bordering on super-human.

In the movie *Lone Survivor,* based on the book by Navy SEAL Marcus Luttrell, the film opens with real-life footage of SEAL candidates enduring Hell Week, five and a half days of brutal physical and mental testing. The men endure around-the-clock operational training, endless calisthenics and running—all while wet, cold, and getting by on minimal sleep. In some of those clips, the candidates are so incoherent with exhaustion, they can barely answer basic math questions from their instructor.

It all sounds certifiably insane until you realize the purpose behind it: to produce soldiers who will not quit in battle, who will not abandon a teammate, no matter how hard things get. *Never quit, no matter how hard things get.* Wow, I was inspired. God was speaking to me, stirring within me the desire to cultivate a warrior's heart. I wanted to become *that guy* who stays strong in the face of challenging circumstances, *that guy* who keeps his cool when everyone else is freaking out, *that guy* whose quiet strength gives comfort to others.

Now, I'm under no illusions. I don't have the raw material to become a Navy SEAL, but that's okay. That's not what God called me to do. However, I can develop the masculine qualities of strength and courage needed to lead my family. And it begins by choosing to confront challenges rather than fleeing from them, to develop within myself the never-quit ethos of a warrior.

In one of those film clips from Hell Week, an instructor tells the SEAL candidates who are tired, wet, and freezing, "Take all this shaking and all this cold, harness it and turn it into aggression." That became a personal mantra for me. Whenever I was tempted to do the easy thing rather than the brave thing, I gave myself a pep-talk. *Take your fear, harness it and turn into aggression.* I'm not talking about being aggressive toward people but mustering the stubborn willpower to stand up and do the manly thing.

So, to all of you guys wanting to rekindle your masculine heart, harness your fear and turn it into aggression. It all begins by choosing to face head-on the challenges you'd normally avoid. I remember distinctly one of those moments in my own life. Megan and I were on a flight heading out west, and the two guys seated directly behind us, who were bound for Las Vegas, were yacking loudly about their upcoming adventures in debauchery. Unfortunately, their conversation was peppered with profanity, and

I could tell their language was getting on Megan's nerves—and mine, too. In the past, I would've kept my mouth shut, all the while reciting Bible verses on meekness to justify my inaction. On that day, however, despite the tremors inside me, I chose to be courageous.

I turned around in my seat and looked at the two guys. With courtesy, I asked them to please tone down their language because I didn't want my wife to hear that kind of talk. To my relief, they immediately turned embarrassed and apologized. I'll be honest; as I sat back down, my vital signs were off the charts. I was still learning how to cope with the stress of confrontation, something I had always avoided in the past. But it was an important step. Little by little, small victory after small victory, I was beginning to develop inner toughness.

That incident ended well. But what if I had turned around in my seat and found two college linebackers who told me to shut up and mind my own business? I'd still hold my head high because I had chosen to step up as my wife's protector. And others who were watching would have seen a man stand up for decency in public, the kind of righteous example our society badly needs nowadays.

And remember, in God's eyes, no battle is insignificant. There's glory in the small victories. As I said before, Megan and I are raising three young boys, and the final hours of the day, from dinner time to bedtime, can be stressful. Mom's tired. Dad's tired. And the kids employ all sorts of passive-aggressive behavior to avoid bedtime. (Parents everywhere understand.) Honestly, there have been evenings when I decided I'd had enough and found an excuse to retreat. "Honey, I have some work to do in the basement. Can you handle the kids tonight?" (Yeah, I know. That's pretty lame on my part.)

Lately, though, I've learned to confront those chaotic evenings as my own personal Hell Week. God is my drill instructor, and I hear him saying, "Take your exhaustion and take your frustration-harness it and turn it into aggression." So, I reach down deep for strength, put on my warrior-face, and I choose to finish the day well. I become a source of strength and encouragement for my wife, not the guy who abandons his teammate in the thick of battle.

I know what some of you are thinking. Getting the kids through dinner, bath, and bed is a far cry from the challenges confronting a Navy SEAL. That's true (although there are days I might disagree), but the glory is in the nobility of the mission. God has entrusted me with the awesome responsibility of leading my family, and when I finish the day knowing they caught a glimpse of Christ's strength and love through me, I feel a warrior's satisfaction. And I think to myself, *It's good to be a man.*

Lord of the Home

So men, stop searching for glory in all the wrong places. God has already bestowed greatness upon you: He has appointed you head of your family (Ephesians 5:23). It is a high calling, an opportunity to exercise noble leadership. God has made you the lord (or master) of your home (1 Peter 3:6), and your wife is your queen.

Despite the howls of modern critics, let us embrace our title with pride, the good kind of pride which is duty-centered, not self-centered. Accept your position with quiet dignity. Hold your head high. When you come home from work and prepare to reunite with your family, let your chest swell with the bigness of what it means to be a godly husband and father. Resist the temptation to shrink away from the demands. Yes, the challenges are hard, but you have a charge to keep.

Let's get practical. What does it mean exactly to say a man is the head of his family? Many of us, unfortunately, have been raised to believe that authority of any kind is all about enjoying the perks, a chance to throw our weight around and get our own way, but that is a distortion of God's design. The truth is, when God gives you a seat of authority, he is entrusting to you a *responsibility.* That's key. When you hear the word *authority,* think *responsibility,* not privilege.

King David of the Bible has something to teach us in this regard. He realized, one day, what godly leadership is all about. "Then David knew that the LORD had established him as king over Israel and had exalted his kingdom **for the sake of His people Israel.**" (2 Samuel 5:12, HCSB) Did you notice the whole reason David wore the crown? For the sake of God's people. He was to employ his power for the nation's good. Imagine having a similar revelation in your own life: "Then one day *[insert your name]* knew that the Lord had established him as head of his home for the sake of *[insert the names of your wife and kids].*"

Isn't this exactly what Jesus taught on leadership, that leadership is about service rather than privilege? "For even the Son of Man came not to be served but to serve others and to give his life as a ransom for many." (Mark 10:45, NLT) So what does it look like when a man leads his family by serving? Keep reading. And prepare to be inspired.

Strong Provider

Men, chances are you are the primary breadwinner in your home. That's no accident. God designed men to provide for their families. We see this truth implied in Genesis chapter three where the husband's primary domain is in putting food on the table while the wife's primary domain is in childbearing and managing the home (Genesis 3:16-19).

Please understand, this is not a slight against families where the woman is the primary breadwinner. I speak in terms of general principles. Because life is messy, the boundaries between the husband's role and the wife's role will often blur and overlap. Each family adapts to its own circumstances. Despite the variations, though, the trendline remains clear. In general, men are hardwired to provide; women are hardwired for childrearing.

So, men, those of you who are out there working by the sweat of your brow, I salute you. You are doing the good thing, the responsible thing. I know some of you travel to jobs every day that are difficult and, at times, downright miserable. You deserve the highest praise of all. Your perseverance shows character, a mark of faithfulness to your family.

It's sad how the malcontents of society sneer at the responsible, hardworking dad as having "sold out" to a conventional lifestyle— as though somehow a man's dedication to his work deserves our derision. Baloney! He deserves our praise. Pulling up stakes and following your dream is not always an option. The realities of the job market often require you to stick with your very imperfect job for the good of your family. That's called life. And as we saw earlier, God praises those who are willing to get their hands dirty, and he elevates them as good examples for others to follow. (See 1 Thessalonians 4:11–12.)

In fact, Paul reserved some stern words for able-bodied people who neglected to provide for their families. He viewed them as deniers of the faith and worse than pagans (1 Timothy 5:8). I'm sad to say it, but many young people in our day are dropping out of the workforce because they haven't found their dream job. The work world, they discovered, can be downright demanding. Listen, I sincerely hope everyone reading these words discovers a job that brings great satisfaction (see Ecclesiastes 2:24), but the responsible man will do his best to provide for his family even in the face of great hardship. It's a mark of character and fortitude.

God bless you, men, for providing for your families. Your example is inspiring.

Spiritual Leader

Is your heart beginning to stir yet? I hope so. And we are just getting started. Brace yourself as we disclose a bit more of the man's glory. "Husbands," writes Paul, "love your wives, just as Christ loved the church and gave Himself for her to make her holy, cleansing her with the washing of water by the word. He did this to present the church to Himself in splendor, without spot or wrinkle or anything like that, but holy and blameless." (Ephesians 5:25-27, HCSB)

Did you notice the passion Jesus has for his bride? He longs to lead her toward holiness so that she stands radiant and blameless before the Lord. Men, that should be your passion as well, that your bride aspires to her highest potential in the Lord. And that begins by setting the example in the home. Your example, men, carries a lot of weight because that's how God wired you. It's all a part of the man's position of headship.

At this point, some husbands are feeling a bit uneasy. "My wife is light-years ahead of me in her walk with the Lord," they say. "How can I possibly lead my wife in the faith?" That's an excellent question. Let's talk about it. First, if that's your concern, I commend your honesty. It's a sign your heart is tender before the Lord. Let that burden inspire your prayers.

Second, even though your wife has a head start in spiritual maturity, you can still encourage her by your example. Here's how: Be growing! Make progress! Consider Paul's advice to a young pastor named Timothy: "Practice these things; be committed to them, *so that your progress may be evident to all.*" (1 Timothy 4:15, HCSB) Men, God is not demanding perfection, but he is looking for diligence in your pursuit of godly maturity. And if your wife has a heart for God, she will delight in your progress.

Third, God appointed you head of the home because you are the man. Period. That's simply God's design for the family. He does not award headship to the one who has the most highlights in his Bible or who has been a Christian the longest. So, don't abdicate your position to your wife or anyone else.

Instead of feeling threatened by your wife's maturity, why not view her as a wonderful asset? In the world of business, the best leaders are *not* necessarily the ones who know everything. Rather, the best leaders accept their limitations and recruit smart people to provide the expertise they lack. They understand that good counsel from bright people is priceless. Rather than feeling threatened by talented people, good leaders embrace them.

In the same way, men, embrace your wife as a wonderful gift. Praise the Lord for placing such an amazing talent on your team. Employ your wife as your most trusted advisor. When the family is wrestling through an important decision, schedule a "briefing." Ask for her insight. Ask if there are passages from Scripture that speak to the matter. Ask if she senses the Holy Spirit nudging her a certain way.

Seeking advice as a leader is not a sign of weakness. It's a mark of wisdom. "Plans fail when there is no counsel," goes the proverb, "but with many advisers they succeed." (Proverbs 15:22, HCSB) Likewise, a husband prospers when he learns to value the counsel of his bride. And many husbands have discovered this important lesson: If you cannot come to an agreement with your wife on an issue, keep working at it until the two of you are unified. It's not about abdicating leadership. It's about valuing the helper and counselor God has provided.

So, as the spiritual leader of your home, take the initiative when it comes to the family's relationship with God. Let the family see and hear you pray at the dinner table. Make sure it's not just mom scrambling to get everyone to church on Sunday. Show them it's important to dad as well. Take to heart what we learned in chapter 16, where we find dad using all of life's ordinary moments to pass along his deep-down love for God.

The Tenderhearted Leader

As we have seen, Jesus Christ embodies strength and courage, but he also embodies gentleness. The man who stood alone against the corrupt religious establishment of his day had such a tender spirit, brokenhearted sinners fell at his feet, willing to bare their souls to his love. In Jesus we find strength and humility melded together.

Think back to that night in the upper room when Jesus stripped down and proceeded to wash the grimy feet of his disciples, something only a lowly servant would ever do. This was the last thing the disciples expected from Israel's king-in-waiting. After washing their feet, Jesus told his disciples, "You call Me Teacher and Lord. This is well said, for I am. So if I, your Lord and Teacher, have washed your feet, you also ought to wash one another's feet. For I have given you an example that you also should do just as I have done for you." (John 13:13-15, HCSB)

Jesus' example serves as a powerful reminder. Men, let us be strong, but let us also be humble and tender, especially toward the family God has entrusted to our care. While the man is head of his home, he must never lord his position over his family. While physically stronger than the wife, he must wield his power only for her good and with Christlike humility. As the apostle Peter reminds us, "Husbands ... live with your wives with an understanding of their weaker nature *yet showing them honor as coheirs of the grace of life,* so that your prayers will not be hindered." (1 Peter 3:7, HCSB)

Those who are steeped in political correctness are likely offended at Peter's suggestion that women, in general, are physically weaker than men, but the truth is obvious to the rest of us: In this world, the woman is the one most vulnerable to oppression. Even the most militant feminist, when she demands equal treatment, tacitly admits by her protests that she speaks from a weaker position.

In no way does the woman's physical weakness imply inferiority, however. Peter has just reminded the husband to show *honor* to his wife. Honor is a powerful word, implying courtesy and deference. A husband should always speak *up* to his wife, never *down* to his wife. Treat her like the queen she is. Remember, both man and woman were created in the image of God (Genesis 1:27). Both man and woman are dependent on each other (1 Corinthians 11:11). And both are equally loved and cherished by our Heavenly Father (Galatians 3:28). Further, God promises to smack down the prayers of the man who treats his wife badly (1 Peter 3:7).

Again, the husband who models the love of Jesus Christ brings a tender heart into the marriage relationship. He knows how to be strong but also gentle. He uses his strength and leadership to look after the needs of his bride. Paul expresses it this way: "So husbands ought ... to love their own wives as their own bodies. He who loves his own wife loves himself; ***for no one ever hated his own flesh, but nourishes and cherishes it,*** just as Christ also does the church." (Ephesians 5:28-29, NASB) Notice how God calls the husband to be just as concerned about his wife's well-being as he is about his own. In fact, the husband is so closely knitted to his wife, his soul is not happy and at rest until her soul is happy and at rest.

During those early years of parenthood when mom is tied down with young children, the compassionate husband wants to know: Is she getting enough rest? Is she getting out and socializing with other women? Does she need to escape for a "mental health day?" Does she have the time she needs to be alone with God and replenish her soul? And this provides the perfect opportunity for the man to imitate Jesus and show his tender side, such as saying to his wife, "Go lie down and rest. Let me wash the dishes." Or "I'll change the diaper." Or "Go out and do something fun. I'll watch the kids for the afternoon."

That's the thing about a truly godly man. He is strong, but he amazes people with his humility, exactly as Jesus did. Men, be the strong leader in your family. At the same time, amaze them with your kindness. Amaze your wife that a guy who is so strong and so courageous is kind enough to tackle a sink full of dirty dishes, humble enough to help with the laundry, and tender enough to wipe away her tears.

And a Christlike dad is tender toward his children as well. The strong father who has callouses on his hands finds pleasure in cradling his infant son. The muscular arms which operate a jackhammer during the day gently hold his young daughter while he reads her a bedtime story. The man who leads a large company, overseeing hundreds of employees during the week, lays on the family room floor on the weekend so his kids can use him as a jungle gym. And he puts aside his electronic devices at the supper table so he can fully engage with his family and thus embody the example of Jesus who longs to enjoy undistracted fellowship with his family around the dinner table (Revelation 3:20).

The Advocate

As we have seen in earlier chapters, Jesus serves as a prayer warrior and advocate for his bride, the church. "Who is the one who condemns? Christ Jesus is He who died, yes, rather who was raised, who is at the right hand of God, ***who also intercedes for us.***" (Romans 8:34, NASB)

Men, let's be advocates for our bride as Jesus is for his. In other words, we speak words only for her good. We don't speak condemnation. It's quite common for men, when they're yacking it up among themselves, to talk disparagingly about "the old lady" at home. Let's be better than that. Let others know of all the blessings your wife brings into your life. And don't poke fun at the weird little ways women are different from men; after all, God made your wife different for a reason: She brings completion to your life. Yes, her emotions work differently than yours. She reasons differently than you do. And she's probably not as mechanically minded as you are. That's all by design! The godly man understands this and values how God created his wife to serve as his beautiful counterpart.

I once had a boss who displayed this bumper sticker on his pickup truck, "I love my wife!" Now that's the spirit of an advocate! What a refreshing contrast to all those grumbling men who like to use their wives as punchlines to their jokes.

Also, becoming your wife's advocate means speaking words of encouragement to her. Let's be honest: It's so tempting in family life to take each other for granted and start sniping, nitpicking, and criticizing. This can become a chronic habit if you grew up in a home filled with criticism. Learn to be kind! Learn to focus on your wife's strengths and express your appreciation for her. Say "Thank you" a lot. Remind her of all the ways she's good to your family. Remember, "Pleasant words are a honeycomb: sweet to the taste and health to the body." (Proverbs 16:24, HCSB) Kind words will nourish your wife's soul.

Finally, Jesus our advocate continually prays for us, so the man who represents Christ in his marriage will continually pray for his family as well. The example of Job, whose biography we find in the Old Testament, inspires me. Although he lived when burnt offerings were central to worship, we can relate to the burden he carried for his family.

> Job's sons would take turns preparing feasts in their homes, and they would also invite their three sisters to celebrate with them. When these celebrations ended—sometimes after several days—Job would purify his children. He would get up early in the morning and offer a burnt offering for each of them. For Job said to himself, "Perhaps my children have

sinned and have cursed God in their hearts." This was Job's regular practice.

(Job 1:4-5, NLT)

What a touching example, how Job continually carried his family, through prayer, to God's altar, seeking heaven's blessing. We ought to do the same.

What can you do to remind yourself to pray regularly for your wife and your kids? If you use a prayer journal, make sure you have a section devoted to your family. Have a family portrait on your desk at work, and let it remind you to keep your family bathed in prayer throughout the day. I met a guy who had a picture of his wife dangling from the rearview mirror of his pickup truck. That's an excellent reminder to pray during those long drives when we have lots of think-time.

Recently I learned a powerful discipline which will keep you praying for your wife as well as keep your heart fully devoted to her. Whenever your mind drifts toward immoral thoughts (an almost moment-to-moment battle for a lot of men) or you start struggling with negative attitudes toward your wife, immediately begin to pray for her. Begin by thanking God for all the blessings she brings to you. Call to mind some of the great memories you share together and thank the Lord for those precious gifts. Consider all the sacrifices she makes every day for the family and, again, praise the Lord for her. Then start praying for her according to her needs. Ask God to help her grow in those areas where she's struggling. Then ask him to fill her heart with the peace and the love of Christ. Ask him to speak to her when she's reading Scripture.

Here's why this discipline is so powerful. This world overflows with all sorts of temptations which can lure our hearts away from our wives. Young attractive girls, scantily clad, are jogging through our neighborhoods. We overhear lurid conversations that get our thoughts heading in the wrong direction. That attractive coworker starts to talk flirty. A risqué ad pops up on our computer screen—and the Devil knows how to use these influences as leverage against us.

But when we use those same temptations as reminders to pray, the Devil's strategy suddenly backfires. Instead of drifting away from our wives, our hearts are rushing toward our wives. Not only that, we are fortifying our families in the spiritual realm with earnest prayer. We become faithful advocates for our families, just as Jesus is for his family.

Godliness is Next to Sexiness

Now we arrive at a truth that is exciting as it is surprising: The strong man with a tender heart is sexy in a woman's eyes. This is not psychobabble; it's age-old Biblical doctrine.

This brings us to the fun part of married love (or the awkward part, depending on how you look at it): the romance and the passion. Yes, God wants you to enjoy your wife and for her to enjoy you. God devoted a whole book of the Bible on the topic, the Song of Solomon. The opening verses dive right in: "Kiss me and kiss me again," says the bride, "for your love is sweeter than wine. How pleasing is your fragrance...No wonder all the young women love you! Take me with you; come, let's run! The king has brought me into his bedroom." (Song of Solomon 1:2-4, NLT)

Some Bible students are uncomfortable interpreting the Song of Solomon in terms of sensual love. Instead, they view it purely as an allegory of Christ's love for the church. My reply? Why can't it be both? As we saw in chapter five *(Love Unashamed)*, God goes to great lengths for us to feel and experience his love. Writers have called our relationship with the Lord a sacred romance. A husband models this sacred romance whenever his wife feels deeply loved by her husband.

This includes the sexual expression of love. After all, God is not shy on the topic as shown in this passage from Proverbs:

> Let your wife be a fountain of blessing for you
>   Rejoice in the wife of your youth.
> She is a loving deer, a graceful doe.
>   Let her breasts satisfy you always.
>   May you always be captivated by her love.

(Proverbs 5:18–19, NLT)

Let's be frank. (After all, it's just us men talking, right?) Maintaining passion in marriage is a challenge, but God wants us to aspire toward keeping those flames kindled. In the passage above, God desires for a husband always to be captivated (*intoxicated*, ESV) by her love.

We men sometimes fall into the rut of being predictable in our habits, including how we romance our wives. And when our wives drop the hint that she'd enjoy more spice in the marriage, we can become defensive. We tend to think romance is "a woman's thing." No, it's a guy's thing, too. All of us were romantic at one time, weren't we? It's called dating. When we were dating our wives, we brought her flowers, sent her cards, took her to nice dinners, thought about her as we listened to love songs, and looked dreamily into her eyes. Unfortunately, we guys are tempted to stop those things once we get married.

Now, I know what you're thinking. Life is busy and it's hard to maintain that kind of intensity. You're right. We can't live in a state of flaming infatuation all the time. Some days marriage is about sticking together and just surviving the latest challenge. But, men, let's not remain there all the time. Let's do what we must to kindle those moments of romantic fun and mutual pleasure.

Once again, may I be blunt? Some among us have given up on kindling passion with our wives and have settled for the ugly substitute of pornography. Others have chosen to flirt with other women or, worse, to pursue an adulterous relationship. All these evils are beneath us as followers of Christ. They are sinful substitutes for true, godly manhood, and they will poison your heart toward the precious bride God has given you. These sins offer fake intimacy when God invites you to true intimacy with the wife of your youth. If you have strayed, it's time to flee these things and burn the bridges behind you. Otherwise, you'll never be able to bring to your wife the romance and affection she desires.

Let's dig down and rediscover the hunger within us to be the charming prince who sweeps Cinderella off her feet. Decide to pursue your wife all over again. Accept the challenge. Channel your energies toward winning your wife's heart like you did when you were dating. Become an expert in seduction. (It's not a sin to seduce your own wife, remember. Go read the Song of Solomon!)

In case you haven't noticed, sex in real life is not quite as easy-peasy as it appears in those highly choreographed and unrealistic love scenes in the movies. To be a good lover, a husband must understand how women in general experience sex and what his wife in particular desires. All of us have something to learn, so why not buy a good Christian book on how to add romance to your relationship or how to spice up your sex life? There are a lot of good resources out there written for Christians, books that are edifying, not sleazy. Order one online if you're nervous about buying it in the bookstore. That way you don't have to explain to anyone what's in the plain paper bag you're carrying.

Yes, it's time to woo your wife again. Impress her. Make her laugh like you used to. Joanne Woodward, who married the very handsome actor Paul Newman, said this: "Sexiness wears thin after a while and beauty fades, but to be married to a man who makes you laugh every day, ah, now that's a real treat." Bring fun and humor back into your relationship.

Remind your wife of all the great reasons she married you. Break out the flowers. Break out the kind words. Schedule the long walks. When you're standing in front of all those Hallmark cards, wondering which one to buy, remember: This is what Jesus does for his bride. He lavishes his love on her (Ephesians 1:8). He takes his bride to the banquet hall so everyone can see just how much he loves her (Song of Solomon 2:4).

Stand Up. Your Father is Passing

Men, this book is called *The Glorious Ordinary* for a reason. God has given you the opportunity to rise to majestic heights of greatness right in your own home. I must admit, though, at times the challenge seems overwhelming, and I'm tempted to fall on my knees like Peter and say, "Away from me, Lord, for I am a sinful man." (Luke 5:8, NASB) Other times I want to go to the bedroom, turn out the lights, and hide under the covers. But do you know what keeps me going? Whenever I catch a glimpse of godly masculinity in someone, my heart swells with inspiration, and I think to myself, *That's the man I want to be.*

Even a strong man of character portrayed in a movie can stir my heart. Recently Megan and I watched the 1962 film *To Kill a Mockingbird*. In my opinion, the lead character Atticus Finch, played with poignant subtlety by Gregory Peck, serves as a beautiful portrait of godly masculinity.

Atticus is a small-town lawyer in 1930s Alabama. A widower, he is left to raise his young son Jem and daughter Jean Louise (nicknamed Scout) all alone. As we watch members of the small town interact with him, we learn that he is widely respected for his integrity, his kindness, and his wisdom. And there's a quiet strength about him. He is, simply stated, an honorable man. If you've seen the movie, you know what I mean.

As the story unfolds, the local judge requests that Atticus serve as the defense attorney for a black man, Tom Robinson, who is accused of raping a white woman. It's an unenviable task, given the racial acrimony festering in the town, but Atticus accepts the assignment. This opens him and his children to harassment by white bigots. Despite all the pressure bearing down on him, Atticus stays true to his convictions and does his best to defend the accused.

Although the movie is a masterpiece of understatement, the trial is spellbinding. Black men and women from all over town crowd into the stifling heat of the courthouse to watch the proceedings from the balcony seats. Atticus' children, Jem and Jean Louise (Scout), squeeze in among them. Once the court is called into session, we watch Atticus, step by step, cross-examine the accusers and disclose the contradictions in their stories. And Tom Robinson's testimony on the witness stand leaves no doubt: This good man has been falsely accused. Despite all the evidence to the contrary, however, the all-white jury returns a verdict of guilty. But Atticus is determined to fight on. He will appeal the decision.

Now comes the moment in the movie that brought me to tears. The court has adjourned, and most everyone has filed out of the room, except for the black men and women in the upper gallery who quietly watch as Atticus gathers his papers into his briefcase. Lost in thought, he does not notice how, one by one, the citizens above are standing to their feet in deference to this honorable man. As Atticus walks toward the exit beneath the balcony, the minister Reverend Sykes quietly urges Scout to her feet. "Miss Jean Louise, stand up. Your father is passing."

Excuse me while I wipe away the tears.

What a tribute to a good man. May the words of Reverend Sykes get into your bloodstream and inspire you toward becoming a truly honorable husband and father. God is with you in this. He will lead you if you stay humble before him. And I pray one day you'll hear these words whispered about you, "Stand up, child, your father is passing."

Men, glory awaits.

Epilogue

Wanted:

Gloriously Ordinary Christians

The idea of writing a book called *The Glorious Ordinary* came to me after I preached a sermon on the topic in our local church, when I was filling in for our pastor. Based on the congregation's positive response, I could tell people were hungering for this kind of message. I was learning just how many Christians, deep down, fear they have nothing big and impressive to offer God and feel relegated to insignificance in the kingdom.

In addition to the congregation's response, two other memorable things happened that Sunday. First, a new couple named Clyde and Arlene had visited our church for the first time. After the service, Clyde told me how much he appreciated the message. For much of his life, he had been carrying around a lot of guilt that went back to his youth. The church he attended as a young man placed a big emphasis on serving God in vocational ministry. In fact, some older members insisted it was God's will that he attend seminary and prepare for pastoral ministry. Deep down, though, Clyde had no desire to enter vocational ministry. He wanted to study engineering. But, as often happens, he deferred to those he thought were wiser in the Lord.

Well, no surprise, seminary was a miserable experience for Clyde, and he dropped out. Eventually, he entered the field of civil engineering, working for the National Forest Service out west, and he thoroughly enjoyed his job. There, he felt God's pleasure. Nevertheless, he carried a lot of guilt for abandoning vocational ministry. He could not shake the feeling, instilled by misguided Christians, that serving full-time as a pastor was the only real way to serve the Lord. When I first met Clyde, he was eighty years old, so he had been carrying all that guilt for decades!

I've met other Christians suffering the same kind of anguish, convinced that only certain kinds of ministries count as real ministry in God's eyes. Because most of us are not gifted to be pastors, teachers, or missionaries, we assume we're God's third-string team sitting on the bench. Or, like happened to Clyde, we get pressured into serving in ways we're not suited.

But God is so much bigger and so much more gracious than all those manmade categories. I pray this book has convinced you beyond a shadow of a doubt that Jesus Christ brings glory to your ordinary. Greatness in the kingdom is accessible right where you are, doing the thing you're already doing, with the talents God has already given you. By faith, we need to see our lives from our Heavenly Father's perspective.

A second memorable conversation happened the morning I preached on *The Glorious Ordinary*. This one occurred *before* the worship service. As people were filing in and finding their pews, I was keeping an eye out for Jack and Barb, longtime members of our church. Jack had recently told me a personal story which I wanted to use in my sermon, and I needed to talk with him briefly to confirm some details.

Here was the gist of Jack's story. Before he and Barb became Christians, they lived across the street from a quiet, unassuming churchgoing family. The dad was not vocal about his faith, but Jack could tell they were devoted Christians. The guy took his family to church every week, and he never mowed his lawn on Sunday. Over time, the family's consistent yet unassuming example proved persuasive. In time, they played a vital role in Jack and Barb's decision to accept Christ.

It was just the kind of testimony I needed for my sermon because it illustrated perfectly how Christ bestows *glorious* significance to an *ordinary* life.

So, as soon as I spotted Jack, I walked over and said good morning. I asked him if I could use his story in my sermon, the one about his neighbor from many years ago. Jack told me he could do better than that. He opened the cover of his Bible and handed me a poem he had been carrying around for a long time, a poem which, I soon realized, was a tribute to his neighbor.

There's something you need to know about Jack. He ran his own asphalting business for decades, so he has the no-nonsense, down-to-earth demeanor you'd expect from someone who made his living in the gritty world of construction; so, I never expected him to hand me a frilly poem, much less carry one around in his Bible for so many years. But there it was!

And once I read the poem, called "Indwelt," I understood why it meant so much to him. It is a fitting tribute to all those beloved followers of Christ who serve as unassuming but persuasive examples in the world.

"Indwelt"
by A. S. Wilson

Not merely in the words you say,
Not only in your deeds confessed,
But in the most unconscious way
Is Christ expressed.

Is it a beatific smile,
A holy light upon your brow?
Oh no, I felt His Presence while
You laughed just now.

For me 'twas not the truth you taught
To you so clear, to me still dim
But when you came to me you brought
A sense of Him.

And from your eyes He beckons me,
And from your heart His love is shed,
'Til I lose sight of you and see
The Christ instead.

Never underestimate the glory Jesus Christ brings to a normal, unassuming life. Our savior has opened the doorway to eternal greatness for all of us. Every one of his children has opportunity to step through and follow that humble, ordinary-looking pathway to glory. And those who do will see their Heavenly Father's smile one day, and they'll hear him say with a heartful of kindness, "Well done, child. Well done. Come, it's time to enjoy your reward."

May God bless you on your journey.

The End

Appendix
Did the Apostles Endorse Slavery?

To some readers, it seems strange if not downright shocking that in chapter thirteen, which deals with the workplace, we're distilling wisdom from messages the apostles had written to slaves of the first century.

The topic of slavery stirs up strong emotions. Not that long ago, historically speaking, America and Europe trafficked in a form of slavery that was especially abhorrent because of its inherent racism. The slave industry relegated millions of black men and women to subhuman status. Thanks to the work of tireless reformers, these same nations eventually abolished slavery and matured to become some of the most tolerant and free nations on earth. But we are still navigating the racial tensions leftover from the past, so when the topic of slavery in the Bible comes up, people get nervous.

To make matters worse, modern critics have accused the Bible of endorsing slavery and, by implication, the ugly sin of racism. While many of these critics have more in common with street-hecklers than careful scholars, they have sown a lot of confusion, and it's important to provide answers to those who have a genuine desire to know the truth.

Really, the best place to go for answers on this dicey topic is the apostles themselves. We simply need to read their New Testament letters carefully and interpret them on their own terms. When we do, we find they were not advocating slavery but providing hope to those bound in servitude. We must keep in mind that, up until recently, slavery has pervaded all civilizations since history began, so we should not be surprised to find the apostles addressing the unique challenges confronting the Christian slave. In fact, there were cities in the first century where slaves comprised the majority of the population! If the apostles had remained silent on the topic, they would have neglected a large portion of the early church.

The slave who embraced the Good News of Jesus Christ longed to know that his station in life did not limit God's purposes for him, and the apostles spoke to that longing with power and clarity: Glory is well within reach of everyone, even the slave. The work of the lowliest slave becomes sacred in God's eyes when performed for the glory of Christ. This was an incredible source of hope to the Christian locked in the lower rungs of society.

Some modern critics remain unsatisfied by that answer. They demand to know, "Why didn't the apostles use their platform to condemn the institution of slavery?" With all due respect to the critics, it's not anyone's business to tell someone else what his life-mission ought to be.

The wise man understands priorities. He realizes there are any of a thousand battles he can fight during his lifetime, but he will amount to nothing if he tries to fight them all. The apostles chose their battles carefully. More accurately, God chose the battle for them, to spread the eternal Good News of Jesus Christ. Because the apostles stayed faithful to the mission, their message has delivered heaven's hope to countless men and women throughout the centuries, whatever their lot in life, whether slave or free.

To suggest the apostles might have overturned the institution of slavery during their lifetimes is naive. Consider the cataclysm required to end slavery in America: The nation nearly destroyed itself during four years of bloody civil war and had to lay on the altar over half a million lives. Yet even the near-apocalyptic violence of the

Civil War was insufficient to annihilate slavery. It also required a profound change in the human heart. And that's where the New Testament played an indispensable role. Through their letters, the apostles planted seeds that would germinate over the centuries and, when the time was right, would give rise to the abolitionist movement. It's no coincidence that God-fearing men and women filled the ranks of those calling for the end of slavery, people whose values were shaped by the message of Jesus Christ.

Consider some of the apostles' influential teachings which would echo through the centuries: Paul poured condemnation on slave-hunting or kidnapping, what we would call human trafficking today (See 1Timothy 1:9-11). Even in the Old Testament, it was a capital crime (Exodus 21:16). Paul implored Christian slave owners to treat their slaves with compassion (Colossians 4:1). He taught that no one should be viewed with contempt based on race, gender, or social status (Galatians 3:28). Peter taught his churches to honor each other regardless of their social standing (1 Peter 2:17). And Paul's compassion toward a runaway slave named Onesimus is forever enshrined in the Bible in a touching letter entitled Philemon, named after the slave's owner. Therein Paul reminds Philemon to treat Onesimus as "a dearly loved brother," not merely as a slave (Philemon v.16).

Again, the apostles of Jesus Christ did not set out to condone slavery; rather, they wanted to provide eternal hope to the slave. And that hope-filled message still speaks today, to the slave as well as to the free—really, to anyone shackled to a role that, from a human perspective, looks like a dead end. In Christ, there are no dead ends. Jesus is the master of turning dead ends into gateways to glory.

(If you jumped to this article while reading chapter 13, please return to page 142.)

If you enjoyed this book and want others to enjoy it too,
please consider writing a review on Amazon.
Thank you!

Personal Note from the Author

Thanks for reading!
I hope *The Glorious Ordinary*
nourished your faith in Jesus Christ.
If you'd like to stay connected,
please visit my website **CheckerspotStudio.com**.
There you can

Contact Me

Comment on the Book

Learn about my other writing projects

You can even contact me
about speaking to your church or church group.

I'd love to hear from you.

–Tim Ferguson

About the Author

Tim Ferguson grew up in Annapolis, Maryland. He worked thirteen years in pastoral ministry in northwestern, Pennsylvania and now serves the Lord as a freelance writer. He also enjoys serving his local church. Currently Tim lives in the Pittsburgh area with his wife Megan and three young boys: Levi, Marcus, and Lucas.

He published his first novel *The God Portal* in 2012. If you haven't read it, you really should. It's available in eBook format or paperback on Amazon.com.

Other Books by Tim Ferguson

(Christian Fiction, available at Amazon.com)

The God Portal

Hopefield

Made in the USA
Middletown, DE
13 April 2019